In the Spirit of Nehemiah

Aaron E. Elliott

Batter my heart, three-person'd God ; for you
As yet but knock ; breathe, shine, and seek to mend ;
That I may rise, and stand, o'erthrow me, and bend
Your force, to break, blow, burn, and make me new.
I, like an usurp'd town, to another due,
Labour to admit you, but O, to no end.
Reason, your viceroy in me, me should defend,
But is captived, and proves weak or untrue.
Yet dearly I love you, and would be loved fain,
But am betroth'd unto your enemy ;
Divorce me, untie, or break that knot again,
Take me to you, imprison me, for I,
Except you enthrall me, never shall be free,
Nor ever chaste, except you ravish me.

-Sonnet 14, John Donne.

CONTENTS

ACKNOWLEDGMENTS

Thanks to Dave Rod, Chris Shore, Doug Perrigin, Tim Ayers, and the leadership of Grace Community Church for granting me a one-year leave of absence to pursue this adventure with God and Nehemiah Vision Ministry.

Thanks to my pastor and friend, Keith Carlson, for which none of this would have happened if not for your belief.

Thanks you to Pastor Esperandieu Pierre, Dianne, Nathan, Charissa, and Lemuel, to opening your home and your hearts to a family of crazy Americans.

Thanks to Geoff Wybrow, whose love and life prepared me more than anything else for my time in Haiti.

Thanks to Jay, Amy, Anna, Jeremiah, Jacob and Fifi Shultz, who we will forever share a special bond of love.

Thanks to Kacie Davis, Aubree Dell, Jim, Cheryl, Janessa and Jaime Warner, Adam Burgraff, Brooke Smalley, E'Tienne York, Brodie Herb, Clerice Attis, Lupson, Michel, and all the staff and NVM family of which there are too many to name.

Thanks to Steve Clark and Jonathan Raves for your technical support and for coming to see us during the year. Thanks also to Kristen and Brian Raves, and to Momma Roush for your time spent with us in Haiti. To the 5 teams from Grace Community Church, and the nearly 1000 other people who we hosted in our year…thank you.

Thanks to our parents who always love our kids so well and are the best grandparents in the world, Jerry and Jane Elliott, John and Diane Hanschu, and Wendy Roush.

Special thanks to Curtis Honeycutt and Sara Sterley, editor-in-chief. Without the initial push of help from Curtis, and the long hours invested by Sara, this work would not exist. Curtis also designed the cover, which is on par with his usual awesomeness.

This book is dedicated to all our partners who supported us in prayer and financially throughout our year in Haiti.

To All of our Financial Partners:

Alison Brown, Amy Fosnaugh, Amy Manley, Amy Miller, Austin and Linda Kirchhoff, Barry Rodriguez, Bob and Pat Pfeifer, Brad & Heather Witter, Brian and Karin Cain, Brian and Kristen Raves, Cheryl Thornell, Chip and Meredith Mann, Curtis and Carrie Honeycutt, David & Megan Schlueter, Denise and Mike Adair, Doug and Ruth Endicott, Eric & Joanne Smith, Gary and Karen Thompson, Grant & Sara Sterley, Greg & Kathy Guevara, Greg & Teresa Overby, Sharon Van Hoozer, Jeff and Sarah Gibbs, Jeff and Krista Davis, Jerry and Jane Elliott, Jim and Donna Meacham, Jocelyn Post, Joe and Tia Bennett, John and Margo Jurgensen, Jon and Deanna Reinoso, Jonathon Raves, Josh and Joanna Burress, Justin and Carrie Gilliam, Karl and Brenda Zachmann, Kathryn McKinley, Keith and Ros Carlson, Ken and Chyrise Ney, Ken and Diane Klotz, Margie Altekruse, Margot and Wilf Bacon, Mark and Sarah Flagg, Michael Jacobs and Mary Jo Norton, Mike and Diane Palma, Nick and Caroline Pease, Patty and Erica Lindley, John and Paula Raves, Phil and Jill Caldwell, Polly Harrington, Richard and Cindy Benedict, Robb and Kim Logan, Robert Hahn, Russ and Michele Luzetski, Sam and Emily Jackson, Steve and Julie Buczkowski, Steve and Susan Clark, Ted and Jennifer Weaver, Terri Richert, Tim and Sharon Murphy, Timothy and Jennifer Tomlinson, Wendy Roush, and Wesley Addington

To All our Prayer Partners:

Kristen Raves, Adam Burggraff, Amy Manley, Amy Osgood, Amy Shultz, Austin Kirchhoff, Barry Rodriguez, Bob Pfeifer, Brad and Heather Witter, Brian Cain, Brian Raves, Carrie Honeycutt, Catherine Bell, Cindy Benedict, Curtis Honeycutt, Dan Altekruse, Dan Oberski, Dana Huckstep, Dave Rodriguez, David Williamson, Denise Adair, Diane Klotz, Eddie Coatney, Emily Jackson, Eness Jarvis, Gary Thacker, Gary Thompson, Grant Sterley, Jane Elliott, Jay Schultz, Jeff Gibbs, Jennifer Weaver, Jerry Elliott, Joe Miller, Joe Reed, Jon and Deanna Reinoso, Jonathon Raves, Julie Buczkowski, Kacie Davis, Karen Benson, Karin Cain, Kathleen Bloxsome, Kathryn McKinley, Keith Carlson, Kevin Roth, Kim Logan, Krista Davis, Laura Plumer, Linda Kirchhoff, Lisa and Joe Miller, Marcus Casteel, Margie Altekruse, Margo Bacon, Mark Lambert, Mary Speer, MaryJo Hein, Michael Leirer, Michael Poorman, Michele Sheets, Michelle Leach, Michelle Luzetski, Mike Mutterspaugh, Nick and Caroline Pease, ORob Childs, Pam Sardar, Pat Pfeifer, Patty Lindley, Phil Caldwell, Polly Harrington, Rena Childs, Ron Stohler, Ros Carlson, Russ Luzetski, Sam Jackson, Sara Sterley, Sarah Gibbs, Sharon Murphy, Sharon Van Hoozer, Steve Buczkowski, Steve Clark, Steve Heiniger, Susie Belford, Ted Weaver, Terri Richert, Yah Buor, and Yvonne Irish.

And thanks to Shelli and the kids for going on such an adventure with God and with me. May God bless us all.

To connect further with *In the Spirit of Nehemiah* go to:
www.facebook.com/inthespiritofnehemiah

INTRODUCTION

The following is a portion of my story of living in the poorest country in the Western Hemisphere following one of the most devastating natural disasters the island of Hispaniola has ever seen. We are a fairly typical Midwestern family of five, except that we lived in rural Haiti for a year. This is our story.

I decided to write this book for a number of reasons. First, it has become a way of talking about what I have experienced this year. This year has been anything but easy. The blessings are probably more than I have ever experienced in one year, but the cost has been great as well. Writing has been good for me to make sense of the year.

Secondly, I have always wanted to write a book. I have started and stopped many times, but never finished anything. Either I found myself saying things that were unoriginal part-way through, I would get bored of the subject, or I just simply lacked the discipline or confidence to finish. I have always felt like I didn't really have anything worth saying. This time I believe I have found something that I can write that is worth sharing. It is my story, and it is the story of God's faithfulness in a very difficult context.

Finally, I am fully aware that our family could never have done this without the support of so many. There are too many to thank by name. Writing this is my way to say "thank-you," especially to those who gave financially to allow us to come. Thank you for your investment. I believe you have invested well. Thank you also to the people who made up our prayer team. We would write a weekly update to this team to share what was on our hearts and to ask for prayer in certain areas. More often than I would like, I would send a mid-week e-mail asking for prayer over the latest crisis. Like the Israelites who would win the battle so long as Moses had his hands raised over the battlefield and needed his friends to hold up his arms (Exodus 17:8-16), this team has held us together. Thank you…our year here was a team effort.

This is dedicated to all those who supported us.

Just prior to leaving Haiti, I read Paul Farmer's book *After the Earthquake*. Paul Farmer has a voice and perspective that I greatly respect. A medical doctor who has served the rural poor for decades in Haiti, Dr. Farmer also has a view of things from the very top, serving alongside Bill Clinton as a special envoy advising the UN and US policy makers on things related to Haiti. He has one foot on the ground serving at a grassroots level and another foot among the most elite in Haiti. His book offers first-hand accounts of the devastating event on January 12th and concludes with Paul offering two very different possibilities for Haiti over the next five to ten years, one more optimistic than the other. I want to believe in the optimistic scenario.

Haiti is a remarkable place, and her people are even more remarkable. The deep faith and perseverance of these people inspire me. There is a great need for the most basic elements for human survival, things like clean water, adequate food, and proper shelter, but there are also great resources in the spiritual and indefatigable will of the people. One key component for the thriving of Haiti is the spiritual will of the people. As more people come and serve the "men of peace" in Haiti, the men of character, the ones who are called to rebuild, as Nehemiah was called to rebuild Jerusalem, then there is reason for great hope! The people of Haiti can indeed rise from the dust of the rubble.

This is our story of serving one such "man of peace" and the ministry God is doing in one part of Haiti.

1 PASTOR PIERRE AND NEHEMIAH VISION MINISTRY

In the Spirit of Nehemiah

Nehemiah Vision Ministry (NVM) exists to help Haitians move from darkness to light, from hopelessness to eternal life (www.nehemiahvisionministries.org). It is a ministry born in the spirit of the biblical character Nehemiah, the man who helped rebuild the city of Jerusalem and the Jewish nation thousands of years ago. NVM began in 2005 in the small community of Chambrun, just outside Port-au-Prince and sixteen miles to the northeast of Toussaint Louverture airport. The vision for NVM was planted in one man's heart about 20 years prior to the ministry's inception in 2005. That man was Pastor Esperandieu Pierre.

In Pastor Pierre's words:

"As a native of Haiti I desire to see the young people grow, to find out their potential, and develop it and fulfill their destiny. If you were to sporadically go to Port-au-Prince and pick up 100 people from ages twelve to nineteen and ask them, 'What is your greatest heart's desire?,' I guarantee 90 percent of them would talk of going to Miami or to New York because many of them feel there is no chance to make it here. You need to get out... And with that tendency they probably will not help. One time I was coming from Indiana, stopping in Miami and spending the night in the Motel 6. It was not that clean, and you know, it could be better. But I did not care because I was there for one night, and I was leaving. Many Haitians feel like, 'I'm here until I can get out of this situation.' With that tendency, you know they will not get busy trying to fix things. So we would really like to teach them, 'you are Haitian and you've got the ultimate responsibility to make things different.' Yes we have partnerships and they are important for us to accomplish our goals, but change will not come until we teach them that it is their job to change it. The Americans cannot change it for them. This is Haiti. You are Haitian. We are trying to teach them and to help them to understand, you are Haitian. We've got a job to do. And it's huge. January 12, 2010, the date of the earthquake, just increased it. Forty-three years old, I don't know how many years the Lord has for me… but I'm looking to invest whatever the Lord has given me, to see if I could impact what is here, to see if my people could see themselves as becoming an element of solution to Haiti, rather than to join the problem. "

This is Pastor Pierre's story of his beginning.

Born into poverty in defiance of voodoo

"I was supposed to be in a building, and most of those who were to be with me died. You know it's got to be God because I could not know in my wisdom that I should plan to be elsewhere that day. I probably would have been sitting right there and would have seen the concrete coming right over my head. But God spared me, and He's got a purpose for that. And the earthquake has caused many things to speed up."

These are Pastor Esperandieu Pierre's words. I have heard his story so many times that I joke that I could tell it to teams if he would rather take the night off. Pastor was supposed to be with his classmates at the university in downtown Port-au-Prince on January 12, 2010. Instead, he was in Trinidad with his oldest son, Nathan. Every one of his 62 classmates who were in the building died when the earth shook at 4:53 PM local time.

But I am getting ahead of the story. Let's start at the beginning. Pastor Pierre was born into a very poor community. His family comes from a region known as the Artibonite Valley, a place that sustains itself mostly by rice farming. His father was on his way to another village to sell his rice one day. He left early in the morning while the sun was not quite up and before the heat of the day would set in, leaving on foot with a donkey to carry his rice, no shoes of course. As the sun would rise, the dirt would heat up, and in the heat of the day, you would find people resting at a well-known crossroads, a place where the river flowed and where many trees offered shade in which to rest. It was here that many women would set up shop to sell a little food for people to eat lunch. And it was also here that this particular day, a team of missionaries came to share the good news of Jesus Christ. Pastor Pierre's father was among those listening to the message that day, and he was moved by the Spirit to give his life to Jesus Christ. This changed everything.

His father was the first one to become a Christian in his entire village after hearing this evangelistic message. The missionaries were wise and followed up with Pastor's father a few weeks after his initial conversion. Their encouragement was key in his faithfulness through very difficult circumstances. Being the *only* Christian in the village made him an instant outsider, especially to a village that was greatly influenced by voodoo. Pastor Pierre to this day takes great care in his own evangelistic efforts to be sure and follow-up with any person who makes a decision to follow Christ due to the difference it made in his own father's life.

The local witchdoctors had a lot of power in this community and warned that if Pastor's parents did not come to them for their voodoo rituals, then they would never have children. You can imagine how their faith was tested when the first two children born to them became sick and died within days of their births. Pastor's blood relative, his cousin, was one of the witchdoctors who was cursing Pastor's parents. The pressures were strong. In this area, there is a strong belief also that if a woman has a miscarriage with more than one child, her womb is cursed and the husband should start looking for another wife because she will never have children.

But Pastor's father stayed faithful. He had learned that "if anyone is in Christ, he is a new creation. The old has gone, the new has come!" (2 Corinthians 5:17). He was not going to have anything to do with voodoo. They stayed faithful, prayed with great fervency, and God revealed to them that if they would boil the water before they gave any to the baby, then the baby would be healthy. Pastor became the third child born, with lots of prayer and the absence of any witchcraft and was named "Esperandieu," which literally translates "Hope in God."

Esperandieu has two brothers and six sisters.

Pastor had a typical childhood for a boy growing up in rural Haiti in the midst of very poor conditions. His days were filled with helping his mother, looking after his siblings, and going to school. Pastor was certainly ornery and had his share of discipline from his father, as you might expect from any young boy, but he did well in school and had the opportunity to go to high school in Port-au-Prince. When he landed in the big city, he only had enough money for the first month of school.

God is Personal and Provider

Pastor always thought of himself as a Christian. His father became a pastor and being a Christian is all he knew. But shortly after he was on his own, he learned that being raised in a Christian family does not make you a Christian. There comes a time when you have to make a personal decision. It was at this time that he heard a message in a chapel service where the speaker turned his world upside down. He spoke from John 1:12, and these words became real and powerful to Pastor Pierre:

"yet to all who received him, to those who believed *in His name*, he gave the power to become a child of God."

Pastor has a Haitian passport. It means he is a citizen of Haiti. But this is just a fact. The truth is that he is a citizen of the Kingdom of God, and he has the power to become a child of God. He doesn't simply belong to the people of Haiti, but belongs to the family of God. Understanding that he is a child of God was the starting point for Pastor for all that God is doing today. As a Kingdom citizen, he has access to the resources of God to become the person God intended him to be.

As a young high school student, unsure of how he was going to pay for school, Pastor began to hang out at a local Christian bookstore. When people would come in and make purchases, he began to help them take their items to their vehicles. One day, a woman had a large number of books, and Pastor helped her carry them to her car. The lady gave him twenty American dollars. That is a huge amount of money to a young Haitian student. He immediately took it in to the owner and explained what happened, and she said that he could keep the money. God was providing.

Pastor is a visionary and entrepreneurial in his spirit, and he has been this way since a very early age. Pastor took some of the money he earned and bought a small camera. All of his fellow classmates were required to provide a small passport-type photo for their school IDs. Pastor started a small business in which he would take the pictures of his classmates and have them printed for a fee, which helped provide for his school fees.

At another time, a pastor in Chicago that was in the same denomination as Pastor's father heard about what Pastor Pierre was trying to do in Port-au-Prince. He offered to pay for his schooling when he couldn't afford it otherwise. I was able to meet this Pastor from Chicago one time and saw how Pastor Pierre was still thanking him. He said that any success he had achieved was attributed to the investment this pastor made long ago. I could see the pride and pleasure in the Chicago pastor's eyes as Pastor Pierre shared these words.

Time and again, God found a way to provide for his schooling until Pastor found himself graduating and earning a scholarship to go to Bible college in Jamaica. When Pastor told his father he was leaving the island, his father wouldn't believe him. It wasn't until Pastor was on the plane and leaving for Jamaica that he finally believed that it was happening.

In the Spirit of Nehemiah

The four years spent in Bible college in Jamaica were exciting and important years. Pastor fell in love and married Dianne, a quiet and soft-spoken woman from Trinidad. She has proven to be an incredible match for Pastor's loud and out-in-front-of-the-crowd personality, helping to provide stability and support. They continue to love and care for one another and are strong partners in the work God has given them.

He also learned so many things that would prepare him for a life in ministry, including a basic construction course. Pastor had built three buildings at the time of the earthquake, including his own two-story home in Port-au-Prince. While most of the homes in his neighborhood suffered great damage or collapsed altogether, Pastor's home and the school buildings on campus at NVM stood strong. Pastor will tell you that God protected them--and that they were properly built.

Towards the end of Bible college, before Pastor's final year, he was preparing to go back to Haiti and start his new life in ministry. It was the fall, and the school was suddenly flooded with all the Haitian students that were supposed to start in the spring. Pastor sought them out and asked them how things were in his hometown. After all, he was getting ready to return. The reports he heard left him with a heavy heart. Politically things were very bad, and there was violence in the streets. The students said he should not return.

One night Pastor couldn't sleep, and he felt led by the Spirit of God to go and read Nehemiah chapters one and two. It was while reading about Nehemiah's heart for his own people and for his homeland that Pastor began to dream about what a ministry could look like in Haiti that was in the same Spirit of Nehemiah. What would it look like to bring the Kingdom of God to Haiti and help the people recover their identity as the people of God? A vision was born, and it was actually put to paper at this time too. Pastor produced a seventeen page document that would later become the foundation for what we know as NVM today.

But as life would have it, the plan was put on the shelf until the season would come for it to be put into action. Pastor was recruited in 1994 to join the staff of Campus Crusade for Christ and was sent to live and train in Kenya for nine months. After completing his training and some time spent in the United States, he returned to Haiti to begin his work with Campus Crusade. His work with Crusade and the Jesus Film project took him all over Haiti, further entrenching his deep passion and love for his people. Eventually Pastor found himself living back in Port-au-Prince and becoming the National Director for Campus Crusade Haiti.

Hurricanes and Chambrun, the time is now

In 2004, two life altering events came together. First, in September 2004 Hurricane Jeanne caused major flooding and mudslides in the city of Gonaïves. 3,006 people were confirmed dead in Haïti, and the death toll in Gonaïves was believed to have topped 2,000. Every building in the city was damaged by the storm, and 250,000 people were left homeless. It doesn't take much for Haiti to have problems with water. With only 1.4 percent of its trees still standing (the rest having been cut for firewood and charcoal), the water gushes off the mountains and causes massive flooding.

It was at this time that a pastor friend of Pastor Pierre's in Gonaïves called and asked if he could help. He knew that he was a part of this large organization in the United States that had access to resources and wondered if there was any way he could come and help out in the crisis. At the time, Campus Crusade did not have a humanitarian arm to help with disaster relief (today they have organizations like the Global Aid Network: www.gainusa.org) that were crucial in leading the response to the earthquake in 2010). Pastor communicated that they could come and do evangelism or counseling and development, but beyond that, they just did not have the resources to help. The pastor on the other end of the phone put a question to Pastor Pierre that would haunt him, "Are four spiritual laws all you have?"

Fortunately, shortly after that phone call with the pastor in Gonaïves, someone from Canada called with $10,000 dollars that had been raised for disaster relief. Pastor was able to collect up supplies and take them to meet the needs in Gonaïves, and thus began the first relief work in which Pastor was involved. His work in Gonaïves laid the foundation for much more work in disaster response ministry.

The second thing that happened was Pastor was introduced to Chambrun. The area is a forgotten place and actually reminded Pastor of the Masai Mara in Kenya. It was filled with tall grass and covered in dust. (If you looked closely, you would swear that you could see a lion crouched down in the grass, waiting to spring on its prey). Pastor had a friend from the community named Gestin who invited him and Dianne out to see the conditions of the community. The name "Chambrun" comes from a French word that means "charcoal," because the community was known as a place to buy charcoal for fuel. What Pastor and Dianne found upon arriving there broke their hearts.

Pastor recognized in Chambrun much from his own upbringing. Some 35 years ago, he was one of those children running naked in a village. The children showed signs of hopelessness, most of them hungry, without clothes, living in mud huts mostly unsupervised, with little or no options for school or a future. And then they met some of the young ladies, thirteen and fourteen years old, attempting to breast feed babies. The babies struggled from hunger as the mothers were barely old enough to feed them, not adequately developed physically. Pastor knew poverty, but he experienced poverty at a whole new level. Having seen what they had seen, Pastor and Dianne could not ignore it.

When Pastor was promoted as the National Director for Campus Crusade in Haiti, the late Bill Bright laid hands on and prayed for Pastor

Pierre. After prayer, Bill asked if anyone had any questions. It was at this time that Pastor asked the question of what national directors should do when their context included great humanitarian needs, where the greatest testimony to the gospel of Jesus Christ is to meet the basic human needs of people. At that time, Bill Bright explained that Crusade didn't have a way to meet those needs. Their focus is evangelism and discipleship. But he went on to say that national directors have the full blessing of Crusade to start things on their own that will serve the work of Campus Crusade in their home country.

So in 2005, Pastor and Dianne began to pray and realized the time had come to dust off the original plan for Nehemiah Vision Ministry. They found the old plans, began to rework them, and then took $200 of their own money and started a small school in the village. A couple teachers were hired, 25 kids were enrolled, and NVM began.

Steady Growth

NVM experienced steady growth for the first five years. By the time 2010 came along, Pastor had acquired some land that was a fifteen-minute walk from Chambrun and managed to build two buildings. One served as the primary school building and the other as a preschool/office building. There were a couple of hundred children enrolled in school. There was a dentist who came twice a year to care for the children's teeth. There was a group of medical professionals, doctors and nurses, that would come twice a year to care for the children's health. Things were growing at a steady and manageable pace.

I was in Haiti for the first time in March of 2009. I can remember sitting up on the top of the mountain that overlooks Chambrun and asking Pastor "what do you see five years from now?" Pastor began to describe a full campus, complete with a church, a school, possibly a hospital, a field for crops, a trade school…a whole host of things. I could practically see it as he described it. "And after five years?," I followed up. "And then we go and do it again in another community. I already have some communities in mind!," he said with great enthusiasm.

On January 12, 2010, the five year plan and steady growth that NVM had experienced suddenly went into light speed as the world responded to the great needs in Haiti. Haiti was the poorest country in the Western Hemisphere before over 300,000 died on January 12, 2010. The needs were great, and now Haiti had the world's attention. I was on the ground five weeks after the earthquake helping facilitate a medical team in many of the Internally Displaced People (IDP) camps. So many people came to help that NVM saw unprecedented growth in 2010. A medical clinic was opened, enrollment in the school grew to 350 children, the church ballooned from 500 to 750 in attendance, a dining hall was built, a warehouse was begun, a project to provide housing for visiting teams was started, and many more things all took place. It was a crazy time.

Whom Shall I Send?

In the midst of this, I was invited to come and help serve NVM by serving as a missions coordinator on the ground in Haiti for one year. The invite was completely unexpected and totally caught us off guard. I had been a pastor at Grace Community Church (www.gracecc.org) for nearly ten years at this point. Grace Community Church has always been a special place for me, a source of great healing and growth in my own gifts and leadership, and I recently became really comfortable with a sense of calling to the local church. I was extremely well cast for my role and was challenged and excited by my work.

My wife Shelli's immediate reaction was "ummm, NO!"

To fill you in on a little background...the first time I met Pastor was over a lunch meeting in the summer of 2008. When people from the church want to introduce our church to the ministry they are involved with, I usually take that call. I was excited to meet Pastor Pierre because he was Haitian, and we have a bias for indigenous leadership when it comes to overseas partners. And he was from Haiti, which I knew was a place of great need for people. As a result of that meeting, a meeting where Pastor spoke with such passion for his people that we had to box most of his lunch up because he didn't stop to eat it, we left knowing we wanted to pursue more of a relationship with Pastor Pierre and NVM.

It was in March 2009 that I was first able to visit Haiti. This time, having heard the stories of how things began, having seen with my eyes the progress and work that was taking place, having smelled the trash in the village and witnessing the life-changing difference the school was making in the young children's lives, I was hooked. I wanted to get the people from my church involved in any way I could. Initially that looked like sending our youth pastor to see if NVM could serve as a site to send a youth team. Our youth pastor went in the fall of 2009, and the relationship continued to grow.

When the earthquake hit, the church was deeply moved by the devastation that was being reported on the news. Because of our growing relationship with NVM, we were able to respond and help in some significant ways. We were able to send two medical teams within weeks of the earthquake. I led the first team in February of 2010. We were also able to help by sending relief food. Kids Against Hunger (www.kidsagainsthunger.org) set up in our gymnasium and close to 1000 people participated in packing food and loading it on forty foot shipping containers that were sent to Haiti. It was a privilege to participate in helping immediately after the crisis.

I was joined by my wife Shelli in leading the third trip we took as a church in July 2010. My wife is a very experienced short-term trip leader in her own right, having taken five or six teams into Guatemala to run medical clinics and do construction projects. She is a pharmacist when she isn't being a wife and mother, and it isn't often that we have an opportunity to lead together. It was while we were leading our team that NVM approached us.

So back to the invitation to move to Haiti. Chip Mann, the acting director for NVM stateside, shared with us that they identified two roles that NVM would like filled by Americans, and then asked us to come fill one of those roles. We talked with Pastor our last night in Haiti, although later he admitted he did not believe we would come. Even though he doubted, he was still faithful to ask. Shelli and I flew home on separate flights from the rest of the team due to some scheduling challenges, and it allowed us to think and pray about this possibility. By the time we landed, we assumed an open hand posture. *As long as God continues to open doors, we will keep walking through them.* This was the attitude we adopted, a very scary position to take I must say.

Over the next four months, so many miracles took place it is hard to account for them all. By August 31st, which was our drop dead date for either getting the approval we needed from my job, or not going at all, I received the phone call. My boss called to say Grace Community Church would be granting me a one year leave of absence. I still remember the exact spot on the road where I was driving with Isabel, my seven-year-old daughter in the backseat, when I took the call. She was the first one I told that we were moving to Haiti, and she cried. Thankfully Shelli, the second person I told, didn't take it quite so hard.

The plan was for us to go and serve for a year, and then I could return to my staff role at Grace Community Church. December would be the date for me to begin my leave. Permission to leave and having the blessing of my local church were the first of many big dominos that needed to fall. When this first domino fell, things moved rapidly. Over the next eleven weeks, many things needed to happen. We needed to raise $60,000 for our plane tickets, living expenses, medicines, insurance, etc. Shelli needed to find out her options with her job as a pharmacist at Walgreens. Would they grant her a leave or have her resign? We didn't know. We needed to figure out what to do with our house. We did not want to sell it with the plan being to return in a year, but could we find someone to live in it? We would be the first family to move to Haiti, so we needed to pack all the furniture and items we would need for our new place in Haiti. And we also needed to set-up all systems and processes by which teams come to NVM, including build a team of coordinators. Did I mention we only had eleven weeks? Or did I mention I would be in India for two of those weeks in October? We needed miracles if this was going to happen, and it was miracles that we got.

Our small group stepped up and said they would help us in our fundraising efforts. Shelli and I invited a ton of people to our house to share with them our story and invite them to support us financially. I think we hosted three of these events, and it was amazing to see the money and the commitments start coming. I also built a team of over 80 people who committed to praying for us on a regular basis. Walgreens was very committed to Shelli, granting her a leave of absence, and her store manager made it very clear that she would like her back in the same store, which is three miles from our house. We had a young man who is like family to us commit to living in our house. My kids know him as Uncle Jonathon, and he is actually the brother of Shelli's sister's husband. Did you follow that? Like I said, how this all came together in such a short time is nothing short of miraculous.

I can remember one phone call from Shelli very clearly. We were down to a few days left to load whatever we could not pack in our suitcases onto a container that NVM was shipping down. We still needed a dresser for the kid's clothes and a table for our new place. Shelli had twenty minutes as she was running from the library to drop the kids off at the sitter before heading to work. She found both the dresser and table for the amount of money she had in her wallet at the time, which was about 20 dollars. They both were packed, along with everything else we needed, on the container and shipped to Haiti.

I am still not sure how it happened. I mean, I know it was a combination of hard work, a good plan, and tons and tons of support from our community. We had open houses, we shared our story of what God was doing, we had many people commit to support us in prayer and financially…and it all came together in time. We landed on the ground in Haiti on December 4th, 2010 with two adults, three children, one family dog, and one of the ten bags we originally loaded on the plane. I hoped the luggage being lost in route was not an indication of how the rest of the year would go!

Not Alone

It turns out we were not the only family on this path. Jay Shultz was asked to fill the role of Director of Operations for NVM. I was familiar with Jay from my work with NVM and had met him once or twice before, but I had not met his wife Amy or their three kids, Anna, Jeremiah and Jacob. Jay and Amy were also in the process of adopting a little girl from the NVM children's home, so moving down would allow them to take little Fedlaine into their home while working to complete the adoption. It was definitely a motivating factor for moving, but not the only one. Jay had always envisioned himself in missions from very early on in his life, and he was excited to join Pastor Pierre in Haiti. Jay had been involved with NVM since the first day it started back in 2005 having served as the chairman of the board until December 2010 and currently serving as the secretary of the board of directors.

When we learned that the Shultz family was considering coming down, we wanted to get to know them. We had many fears that seemed natural…what if this family was awkward to be around? What if we didn't get along? What if their kids were super annoying? We went to their house the first time for a cookout with all of these questions running through our minds. Shortly after we arrived, Anna, their sixteen-year-old daughter took our girls to meet her horse. She was instantly cool in my girls' eyes. It was quickly clear that these were great people that we would love to live and work alongside.

The Shultz family became a big chapter in our story of living in Haiti.

The Adventure Begins

On December 4th, we moved in with Pastor Pierre and his family. They were incredibly gracious and hospitable hosts, and our kids loved being there. One of my first tasks was to get our "house" set up out at Chambrun, a circus like tent that would cover much smaller tents that would serve as our rooms. We lived with the Pierres for two weeks, and the adventures began almost immediately after landing. Little did we know what was to come.

2 THE ROCKS CRY OUT

History

I did a lot of reading over my year in Haiti. The sun goes down early and when the kids had all settled in, there were not many distractions. The internet is slow, there is no TV, I can't hang out with my neighbors around the fire pit, so I read. A lot. One of the subjects that I chose to study was Haiti. Having previously read *Mountains beyond Mountains* by Tracey Kidder, I started with Graham Greene's *The Comedians*, a work of fiction set during the reign of Baby Doc. It gave a taste of what life was like under a brutal dictator, and left me feeling like any good comedy would, as if all the characters are fools. Next I came across a self-published book called *Travesty in Haiti* by Tim Schwartz. It served as one of the most insightful resources I encountered into the challenges of development work in Haiti. Tim is an anthropologist who tells his story of working in Haiti for ten years. Unfortunately, the book ends with a very hopeless tone, and it took me a solid couple of weeks to climb back out of the internal funk it helped create in me. Challenging and educational, *Travesty* was one of the best books I could have read. And then I read *Haiti: The Tumultuous History - From Pearl of the Caribbean to Broken Nation* by Philippe R. Girard, which was the most informative book on the history of Haiti that I read.

One of the key themes in Girard's book is how the thread of poor political leadership has affected Haiti since it first became an independent nation in the late 1700s. Haiti has had leader after leader who have lined their own pockets at the expense of their people and who sought to retain their own power at the expense of their opponents. This lack of leadership on behalf of the Haitian people contributed greatly to Haiti becoming the poorest country in the Western hemisphere. Little did I know that the week we arrived, Haiti was voting on a new president. I had no idea the historical significance of this election, or the impact it would have on me and the Haitian people.

Tires Burn

We had just returned to Pastor's house from Chambrun. I was spending my days working alongside our staff building our tent/house. It was quite a shift from the first snowflakes falling the day we stepped on the plane at home to working outside in the sun all day. I was sunburned, tired, and dropping weight (which was really a good thing). There was a team on campus, a really competent team of guys, and two of them returned to Pastor's house with us this evening. The plan was to have them spend the night with us at Pastor's house in order to get up early and work all day at the house helping Pastor with a project. It would be the first of many lessons on how plans change.

This first night was the night they announced the presidential election results. Nineteen candidates had run on the ballot, and an outright winner would require 51 percent of the vote. There were three favorites. Mirlande Manigat was the clear frontrunner. She received a percentage vote somewhere in the mid-thirties. The next two candidates, Jude Celestin, the current president's pick, and the people's man, Michel Martelly, or "Sweet Mickey" as he is called, were neck and neck. It was quite a contrast of characters, really. Mirlande Manigat is a former first lady, very well-educated, and favored by many of the wealthy and educated. Jude Celestin was not very popular among the younger generation, but very well-funded and backed by the current president, Rene Preval. Michel Martelly is a bit of an outsider, a singer and entertainer that was beloved for being the self-proclaimed president of Kompa music. It was announced that Jude Celestin had just edged out Martelly.

Pastor said all the candidates were rallying their people and that the election results were tampered with by the current president. Celestin should not be in the run-off with Manigat. We should expect the unexpected tomorrow, according to Pastor.

When we woke up the next morning, we could see smoke rising all over the city. Pastor's house is located in Tabarre, just down the road from the US Embassy. It is a fairly secure area and not far from Port-au-Prince. From the roof, we could see black smoke all over the place. Pastor said the people were burning tires and the city was basically shut down. We spent that first day laying around reading, playing with the kids, occasionally watching the smoke from the roof, and catching up on writing our blog, although the internet was not working. We were safe and secure, and we rather enjoyed a slower day that first day with all the other changes we had recently experienced.

At midday of day two, we took one of the staff members from one of our partner ministries to the airport. They had been stuck at Pastor's house due to the protests. The major airlines were not flying, but he did manage a flight to the Dominican Republic, so we headed out to the airport. It was eerie driving on the streets. There was hardly a vehicle to be found, and gone were the typical throngs of people walking along. You could see at just about every intersection the smoldering of burnt rubber from all the tires that were set on fire. Towards the end of day, we decided it was time to take the two men back to Chambrun. Pastor knows most of the police and has many contacts along the road from his house to Chambrun, and the reports were that things were calm. So we decided to take Jeff and Don, the two men that were stranded at Pastor's house, back to join their team in Chambrun.

Heading to Chambrun

Nathan and I headed out in the red Ford Ranger with Jeff and Don in the pick-up. The sun was not yet down, and we wanted to try and get there and back before dark. As we left, we encountered the same atypical traffic pattern as earlier in the day—hardly a vehicle in sight. In fact, as we turned on the main road, there were makeshift roadblocks going up. I had to drive up the right side of the curb during one section so as to avoid the rocks in the middle of the road.

As we turned right at Carrefour Marrassa, typically a very busy intersection with a market and a common tap-tap stop (a "tap-tap" serves as public transportation in Haiti, usually a modified pick-up truck or bus that is brightly painted and decorated), we encountered another makeshift road block, this one built out of some kind of metal. Jeff, never short of energy, decided he would hop out and just drag a piece out of the way so that we could pass through. There was a deep ditch on the side of the road, so driving around it was not an option. Jeff made quick work of clearing a path, and as he rounded the back end of our truck towards the back door on the passenger side, I suddenly saw his feet slip up over his head in my right rear-view mirror. Just as he was reaching for the door, he slipped on some oil in the road and totally wiped out. From the shadows of the wall at the nearby building, we heard about twenty Haitians erupt with laughter. We didn't even know they were there until they cracked up laughing at this *blan* (white person) wiping out in the middle of the road. It was funny, but also a little unnerving to know there were that many Haitians standing off in the shadows where we couldn't see them.

Jeff was a little scraped up on his elbow and leg. Although I think his pride was hurt more than anything, he was bleeding from his arm. We continued on our way only to come across a barrier that we could not maneuver around. There was a large fire burning in the middle of this one. We found out later that someone had set a UN vehicle on fire at this intersection. At any rate, we turned around and took a back road. It was bumpy and slower, but we made it back to Chambrun without incident. We said hello to some of the people on campus that we had not seen in two days, let them know what we were seeing, and then Nathan and I started to load up to head back.

There is a very distinct memory I have at that time. We were right near the gate, about to head out, and I stopped the truck and asked Nathan if he had a cell phone. I had not yet purchased a cell phone myself, and I wanted to know we could call someone if we encountered any trouble. I had only been in country a couple of weeks, and Nathan was only sixteen, albeit a strong, physically imposing sixteen-year-old. He reassured me that he had his phone, but I was still a little nervous heading back.

We were making good time. We went back the bumpy dirt road. We came out just near the spot where Jeff had taken his spill. Unbeknownst to us, Pastor was sitting just to our left a little way up the road. He had been trying to call us and didn't know that we were taking the back road. We continued on our way and came upon a tap-tap that was turning around in the road. I was already a little on edge because it was getting very dark, there was hardly anyone around on what is a normally packed road, and why were all these people out of the tap-tap and in the middle of the road? We continued on slowly. As we pulled up to the spot where I had to go around the road block by driving up the curb, I realized that they had rebuilt the road block all the way across. It immediately clicked.

"Hey Nathan, I think they rebuilt the road block."

Right as I began to utter these words, I noticed from my peripheral vision that something was heading right towards us, and it was not coming in a friendly manner. There were giant pieces of concrete and rocks suddenly coming at us from multiple directions. The first one I noticed from the right side. The next one came from behind a cement wall on our left. I was forced to make a split second decision: slam on the brakes and head backwards, or slam on the accelerator and continue through the barrier. My reaction was to gun it.

"Nathan! Hang on!"

Fortunately I have one of those brains that usually does not lock up in these types of moments. I typically get very focused and very decisive. I immediately slammed the accelerator, hoping that my quick change in speed would cause those throwing at us to miss. I realized the smallest rocks that made up the barrier were the ones to the left side of the road up on the sidewalk. I quickly jumped the curb and headed straight for the barrier. Just as we got airborne, jumping the barrier, crashing down the curb, I saw a giant rock come from the roof of the three-story building on our left.

The rocked slammed down on our roof, just on the rear end of the cab where the rear glass meets the roof.

Nathan and I were clear.

The adrenaline was pumping now, and we were flying. Nathan suddenly yelled "THE TURN! THE TURN!!" I slammed the brakes, and we screeched for probably twenty feet to a stop. I threw it into reverse and screeched back to the turn. We turned left. As we continued our drive, we realized that the roads were clear from here on in. We were on the road that passes directly in front of the US Embassy, where certainly no one would be throwing rocks at us. We tried to get our heart rates to slow as we made our way back to Nathan's house, hardly believing what we just experienced.

Without a Voice

Pastor returned shortly after we did. I showed him the new dent in his truck and relayed the story. He shook his head and was very grateful that we were okay. He shared with us that he got word they were throwing rocks and had been trying to call us. He was waiting along the road we were supposed to be traveling to catch us and take us a back way. The incident never should have happened. He was very disappointed that it did and also very thankful we were okay.

Shelli and I were very slow to share this story with people back home. We had not been in country two weeks yet, and the reports back in the states of what was taking place with the protests were really, really drastic. You would have thought the country was in complete anarchy if you read what the news was printing. People were worried enough about us, and we didn't want to contribute to their worry. So it didn't feel right to tell everyone I had rocks thrown at me, especially when the incident really should have been avoided.

Plus, how would people perceive the Haitian people when they find out that they are throwing rocks at whoever is passing by? I am a *blan*, working under a Haitian-led Non-Government Organization (NGO) that exists to help the very people who are probably throwing the rocks. I can easily see that people back home would read my story and think, *why would I send money or anything to help these people? Look what they are doing. Is this how they engage with their own political process?* I did not yet have any understanding of the context, but my gut told me that my supporters would interpret this event as I told it from their own context and miss the complexity of the situation that led to the protests and the rock incident.

Pastor knew who the people were that were throwing the rocks. I am not sure he knew them personally, but he knows everyone along that road. They all know his red truck too. He has been driving it along that road for over a year now, every day. He could easily find who it was that was doing it. I wanted to go confront them, let them sit face-to-face with me and explain to them that what they were attempting would not serve any positive result for them. Pastor wasn't having it.

This very well may have been some young kids who were looking for an excuse to cause some trouble. I was a kid who used to throw mud balls at passing cars in our neighborhood at one point in my childhood. Of course, we just thought it was a fun challenge to see if we could hit the cars, and double exciting if we caused someone to get mad enough to stop and chase us. We never wanted to cause any real damage. But I wonder what mentality I would have had if I was fueled by a sense of hopelessness or frustration. Could I have been one of these kids throwing rocks?

Or it may have been very serious-minded individuals who were outraged by a corrupt political process and lacked any creativity or outlet to voice their frustration. Most likely they were people with little education and few options. I mean, what would I do if I had no voice? What if I had no say? What if I was living in the context of at least 80 percent unemployment, in a tent camp, with no food, no clean water, no access to education, and basically without hope? I might easily be sucked into throwing some rocks with my buddies. When a person lacks due to poverty, they just don't lack physical resources, but they also lack imagination. Throwing some rocks was maybe the best they could imagine for getting some attention.

Resolve

Due to pressure from the international community, the Haitian government did get it right. A run-off was held in early 2011 that put Manigat against Martelly. The president's man, Jude Celestin, was out. Martelly won easily in a vote that was widely criticized, but the process was not perceived as corrupt enough to negate the results. President Martelly peacefully took office on May 14, 2011.

I did not expect to have my perseverance tested as early as I did in our year. How would I let this incident shape my thoughts on Haiti, and my year here? The incident certainly was scary. What would have happened if the rock that hit our roof had come through our windshield and one of us had been injured? How would I explain that to Shelli, or to Pastor if it had been Nathan? I resolved to claim three things in my heart:

1. God has called us to come here. We are not leaving before our appointed time short of something forcing me to go home. If He has called us, He can continue to look after us and I will trust that I am here for the year, whatever comes my way.

2. I have much to learn here. I will try and learn all I can about the causes of what leads someone to throw rocks at a passing vehicle. I will

withhold judgment of this incident until I understand possible underlying causes

3. I will choose not to live in fear. I will certainly be more aware and more on guard as I drive through town.

Thankfully I did not have any more rocks thrown at my truck, although this was certainly not my last adventure behind the wheel of a vehicle in Haiti.

3 CHOLERA

Water

Water is really, really important. Two-thirds of our body weight is made up of water. A human can go weeks without food, but go more than one day without water, and you are in big trouble. Estimates vary considering many environmental variables, but the range is from two to ten days for how long someone can live without water. Before coming to Haiti, I never really thought about water. I mean truthfully, water is everywhere back in the States . Okay, maybe every now and then when the summer has been hot and we are low on rain and the powers-that-be restrict the days I can water my lawn, but other than that, I don't think a lot about my water; it is just there.

If I wake up in the middle of the night thirsty, there in my bathroom is clean, safe, drinkable water. There at my kitchen sink is what seems like an endless supply. Turn the other knob, and it comes out hot! Go to any public building and you find a drinking fountain somewhere accessible where you can have water at no cost. And of course if you can't find the endless free options, there is now just about every variety of water you can imagine available in little plastic bottles for you to purchase. The US is flowing with water.

I never really noticed before how the water freely flows where I am from. But I notice now because in Haiti, many hours are spent nearly every day in the acquisition or maintenance of clean water. I went to places in the mountains where people actually walk up to five miles every day just to get their water. While living in a tent for three months, I would shower in cold water every day, and the water that would come out of my showerhead was not safe to drink. What a contrast from the hot drinks that were available to me in my showerhead back home (I'm not saying I always drink the water in my shower, but it is a viable option).

Cholera is a reality in Haiti. We knew this before we moved and Shelli, of course, being the medical professional that she is, did her research on it. Cholera is a caused by a bacterial infection of the small intestine. You get it from drinking water that is contaminated, or eating food that has the bacteria. Most of the time if you get cholera, you don't get very sick. Only one in twenty people are usually severely affected, and of those who are severely affected, most get better if properly hydrated. If you do get sick and don't get treated right away, severe diarrhea and vomiting causes severe dehydration, and a person can die within hours.

Frankly, I never worried that much about cholera. Shelli knows how to treat it, and we have nurses on campus that can help us. In Chambrun's immediate vicinity, there had not been a breakout of cholera. In Haiti, you have to be a specially-licensed treatment center to treat cholera, which our clinic is not. So anytime we had someone come in who we thought may have cholera, we would get them started on an IV to hydrate them, and then send them off to the nearest registered clinic. We have only confirmed one or two of those people that we sent off as actually having cholera because most of the time the people didn't come back to let us know if they actually had it or not.

Knowing what I do about cholera, and knowing how good our nurses living on campus are, cholera never frightened me. Well, it never frightened me, that is, until I witnessed its effects on an entire community firsthand.

A Call for Help

Pastor is well connected here in Haiti. One of his connections sends him information from all over the country via e-mail. On this particular day, he got word that a mountain village called Bouzi was having a cholera outbreak. We just so happened to have a team from a school district near Ft. Wayne, Indiana that was here to work on water treatment issues. Teachers and students had a water treatment set-up with them that could be installed in this little village and purify their water. It was decided that since we were so close--maybe an hour drive through the mountains--we would go check it out and see if we could help.

We packed up three vehicles, two Toyota Land Cruisers and one of our Ford Ranger pick-up trucks. We took some ten liter jerry cans that we were given to distribute so people would have nice containers to transport water. Having nice, clean containers to carry your water is a real blessing. And we basically took all the right people who could look at the situation and determine if we could help. We took an engineer who knew all about properly treating water, some of the key science teachers, and also a nurse from one of the teams. I was one of the drivers behind the wheel of one of

26

the Land Cruisers.

One of the joys of my time in Haiti was driving. I tell people that I was made to drive in Haiti. For some reason, I just get the systems and flow of traffic. Maybe being aggressive comes naturally behind the wheel, I am not sure. But I love driving. When I drive through town, I honestly prefer the pick-up trucks over the Land Cruisers. The Land Cruisers are geared low and don't have much pick-up when you want to go. I frankly didn't care to drive them much. Well, my opinion quickly changed. I learned what the Land Cruiser was made for. The roads we drove, if you could call them that, were steep, narrow, made from rocks, sometimes washed out, winding, treacherous, and downright scary at times. Someone in my truck commented that people back home would pay a lot of money to have an opportunity to drive on roads like this. That Land Cruiser was a dream to drive. Shortly after we left, I realized four wheel drive was a necessity and felt that rush of joy as I slid the shifter back engaging the front driveshaft. It was geared perfectly for the small water crossing followed by the steep uphill climb through mud. It was just right for grinding down a slope only to take a hairpin turn near a cliff and immediately start climbing. In a word, it was awesome. And I now had a new favorite vehicle, for mountain driving anyway.

We literally took the road to its very end, only stopping a few times along the way.

Church is Everywhere

The first town we came to, right there on the road was a little church where the pastor was running a school. Pastor Pierre quickly made introductions and asked about the cholera situation. The local Pastor explained that they were fine where they were, but if we kept going up the road we would find the next village was having issues.

Now really, at this point we were in the middle of nowhere, after an hour of driving on some of the most treacherous roads I have ever seen. The roads were barely passable for our vehicles, and mostly we saw people on donkeys, not other vehicles. And yet, planted up in the mountains, right in the middle of this tiny mountain village, is this little church. And that was true of every little village we came into. I had heard big-name preachers talk about how the church is the best resource to combat the great Goliaths of the world, or the church is the hope of the world, or insert whatever euphemism or comparison you want, but here I got a little taste of that reality. If someone wanted to make a difference in one of these tiny little communities, I think I would start with the pastor at the local church. This is where the community apparently gathered.

Water Sources

The first water source was just down the road from the first town. It was actually pretty sophisticated. The government or some big NGO had been through and taken their mountain stream and converted it to a pretty nice set-up. There were numerous spigots all around to turn on and off, and there were even outdoor concrete showers. Someone had clearly done some significant work. Many from the community were gathered around the shade of the nearby tree, and it was rather a pleasant afternoon. Pastor drew my attention to the hill and pointed out how easy it would be for this water source to become contaminated. There was a shepherd with a flock way up the way, and if he bent over and did a number two on the hill, and if it was contaminated with cholera and then flowed down hill with all the water and got this whole water source contaminated, then the whole community would be in trouble. I could picture it, and up here in the mountains, this was the only water source.

We got back into the vehicles and drove a few more minutes to the end of the road. We walked through a small market, up a narrow hillside, through a dry river bed, and up another little way to the edge of a mountainside. Hidden away in the side of the hill was a small stream, much like a spigot. Here was the other water source for the entire area. It was low to the ground, constant in its flow, but you could only get a small bowl under the river rock where it flowed. People were lined up all around, getting water from this drip, dumping their smaller bowls into larger containers (many of them buckets), and then carrying them off to wherever they lived. It was a good seven minute walk from the market area, and at least that far from where anyone lived. And then it probably took what seemed like ten minutes to fill just one five gallon bucket. This again was the only source of water for the small community that lived there.

We walked back to our vehicles and then walked in the other direction down a narrow pathway. Again, we passed a church on our right where some sort of service was taking place. Just a little further down the road we came upon the cholera clinic. This was the first cholera clinic I would set foot in, and it wasn't much. There was a makeshift tent set up next to a small concrete building. Inside the tent were nine cholera cots. A cholera cot is a regular army cot, a few feet off the ground, with a hole cut where your backside would hit, just big enough for it to fit through. I saw a young boy with his bum hanging through and a bucket underneath. I saw a few other patients, all on IVs, all looking very tired and worn. I saw another older gentleman, completely naked, and clearly in pain, with no IV set-up. He looked on the brink of dying to me. This was awful. This man may not make it a few more hours!

We got word that they couldn't get an IV started on this gentleman; his veins kept collapsing. Apparently this little clinic was being run by one gentleman who was doing the best he could with the resources he had. He had seen as many as 130 patients the previous week, and a few of them were too far gone and unable to recover. A few people had already died. Around the corner of the cement building I met a small family, a mother and three kids, all who were being treated with oral rehydration. I thought of my young kids back in Chambrun, as I looked at these little ones that were about the same age as my own.

Another thought came to my mind next: After seeing their water source, and now seeing their clinic, I couldn't help but think, what if water, the very thing you need for life, actually becomes your enemy? What if the water you are drinking actually tries to kill you?

Trying for a Stick

When we got word that the workers there could not get an IV started in the older naked man, we asked if our nurse could give it a shot. I wondered if they had truly given up or not, but we had just gotten there, were feeling helpless, and perhaps this was at least something we could do. We could try and get an IV started, which would most likely save this man's life. Many of us started to quietly pray, and our nurse went to work. You could feel the nervous hope and expectation among our group and the urgent prayers to please let her get this IV started.

I am not sure how many times she tried, but each time she did, the same result occurred. A few moments would pass when we thought she had it, and then the vein would collapse. It was frustrating to say the least. Not many times do you feel like a person's life is hanging in the balance. Our nurse, after trying for a while, finally stepped back, but the small Haitian staff kept trying. Thankfully, eventually, an IV was started and the vein held. This man started to receive the life-saving rehydration he desperately needed.

I am not sure I had ever heard of cholera before coming to Haiti. In the US, it is so rare that I can't ever remember even hearing about it growing up as a kid. But here I was, standing on a mountainside, watching these poor people, many of them children, suffer from a little bacteria that literally dehydrates your body to the point of death, sometimes in just a few hours. This little clinic was treating up to thirty patients a day at the time we got there. It was hard to explain what it felt like being there. The best word I could come up with was sacred. Sacred as in you walk softly, like there is a great deal of respect for the dignity of the people, even as this disease was attempting to strip it away. Sacred in that life and death seemed to hang in the balance. Sacred is the best word I could come up with.

Improvement

It was amazing to see how much the older man improved in the short time we were there. He went from looking like being on the doorstep of death to peaceful. Color returned to his face and the life that appeared to be slipping away was returning.

We devised a plan that day. We left half our jerry cans with the clinic to distribute as they saw fit. The other half we drove the short distance to the other mountain town and left them with the pastor we spoke with earlier to distribute as he saw fit. A smaller group would return in a few days to install a water treatment device and a 600-gallon tank. The device would work off a small battery that was recharged by a small solar panel, and as long as the people could bring water to the tank, they could treat it and offer clean water to the community.

The next week Pastor got a new report. It said that the cases of cholera in that area went from over 130 the week before to under twenty the next week. I am not sure that the team who raised the funds and installed these systems ever heard how their work literally saved lives in the small mountain town of Boozi. But I know none of us who saw that clinic will ever forget the impact of cholera on a community.

An Encounter with Jesus

I think Jesus understands the value of water. When he encountered an outcast woman at the well, at midday when the sun is at its peak and the rest of the people are under shade, he offered her living water, the type of water where she will never thirst again. Read the story in John 4. This story came to mind after our day at the clinic because I think Jesus understood and cared about whole people. Not only does Jesus care about the spiritual needs of people (like the poor woman at the well), but he cares greatly for the physical needs of people. I saw this in action this day. We offered people clean water and restored health and did so in the name of the One who offers living water.

4 GIFTS

Every good and perfect gift is from above…
James 1:17.

Birthday on the Mountain

As soon as my oldest daughter Isabel realized that we would be in Haiti for her birthday, she declared she wanted to celebrate by hiking a mountain. I think she got the idea from me talking up the good parts of moving to Haiti. I figured a seven-year-old from Indiana would love seeing mountains, so I was talking them up during our preparations to move. I couldn't make hiking a mountain happen on my own, so I asked Pastor Pierre to show us the best place for our family to do some birthday hiking. Pastor is incredibly conscious about safety, so he decided to be our guide. So on January 10th, Isabel's birthday, we got in the truck and drove up the dirt road to the aptly named Goat Mountain, about five miles outside Chambrun.

The hike itself was just right for little Isabel's legs. Even our youngest, Sitota, could manage, although he enjoyed much of it from my shoulders because he prefers to ride "on top" of Daddy. Our hike wound up and down parts of the mountain, which was perfect, and we soon arrived at our destination. Isabel suggested the mountain should be renamed "thorn mountain" due to the number of thorn bushes she observed. Pastor Pierre was leading us to introduce us to some people who live on the mountain and attend our little church.

As we came down the path, there were three homes in a row—two next to each other, the third just a little further down the path and to the right, and a fourth home a short walk up the mountain. The path divided the homes from the slope of the mountain, where their trash dump covered a large expanse. Bottles littered the hillside like a plastic graveyard. One of the roofs featured an old, open suitcase worn out by countless days being battered by rain and having the sun's heat beat down on it.

The houses were triangular lean-tos with straw and grass roofs. "These are four of the most rustic, crappy houses that I've ever seen," I thought to myself. This was Clement's joupa, which translates in Creole to "shack" or "hut." Clement works as one of the daytime security guards for NVM. He is a man of simple means—bald, average height, and strong, but not muscular. For a guy who shows signs of hard living, with lines on his face and skin that offers clues to his age, it is evident that he has been living his entire life in the Caribbean sun. But Clement has lived well—well enough to be getting along in years.

Clement was thrilled to have us come visit his home. "Please, come in, come in," he offered in Creole, his voice quiet and very sweet. He invited us in to his joupa, where we sat on the bed. His three kids were also glad to have us in their hut, but they were shy, hiding behind their mother, Illomene.

Clement and Illomene are together, but they are not married. Clement wants to build a proper home with his money before he marries. I found this is very common among the Haitians that I met. A proper home is a big priority over and above what my Christian tradition would call a proper relationship between man and woman who have children together. When I inquired the names of Clement's children a few weeks later, I was told his youngest daughter is called "Tifi," which means "little girl." He needed to go home and ask Illomene what her real name was.

I guess until he gets a new house built, the five of them live here.

Once inside, per Clement's request, Pastor Pierre uttered a prayer of blessing for Clement and his family that was beautifully honest. "Father, we thank you for Clement and his simple house, and this simple bed where he and his wife lay down at night. It is a simple home, and Clement works hard to provide for his family. We ask that you bless the work of his hands. We thank you that he knows Jesus as his Lord and Savior and that he has the eternal hope of salvation with you. We thank you for the joy that you have put into his heart that can never be taken away. We pray your continued blessing and protection over this house and over his family. We pray you will continue to provide all his needs and for the needs of his children, through Jesus Christ our Lord. Amen."

Pastor prayed in English, so Clement didn't understand any of it, but Pastor was able to name the truth of the situation without a hint of demeaning Clement and his family. He recognized Clement's dignity and value, and the words came without the slightest pause or hesitation; they flowed from a deep well of compassion and understanding somewhere inside Pastor Pierre. At the moment he prayed that God would bless this man, who I was learning was already blessed in many ways, all I could notice was all that Clement was lacking. I was afraid the bed would crumble to pieces as I sat on it, and the straw roof would leak every time it rained.

Clement rarely stands fully upright. He usually bows his head to the side, a sign of submission and deference in Haitian culture. Clement is expressive, if not a little goofy. As we left his house, he started to sing and dance. His joyful spirit is infectious, and as we exited his home, he blocked our path with dancing and singing. We couldn't leave until we all joined in with him, and I quickly found myself dancing with joy, kicking my feet out in playful exuberance with Pastor and Clement.

From where we stood, you can see NVM's campus in the distance, a solid hour walk when the way isn't turned to mud from the rain. Getting water is also a considerable hike, with the closest water source a twenty-minute journey. I have heard it said that you have not experienced poverty until you have smelled it. Well, these people were poor. Sydney, my five-year-old, piped up, "It smells up here." Sometimes I am so thankful for the language barrier and that our Haitian hosts could not hear my daughter's honest yet potentially embarrassing comment. She of course was right. All their trash was heaped in a pile right in front of us, and I didn't notice a bathroom anywhere.

Sizing up the situation, Pastor Pierre spoke gently to me, "This is really bad up here. We need to get these people some tarps for their houses." When Pastor says something is really bad, it must be really bad because this is his world day-in and day-out.

We finally headed out to finish our walk around the mountain, Clement now part of our hiking expedition. We found a nice place on the other side of an abandoned house where we could be alone as a family and let Isabel open some presents we brought for her. She got a Cinderella Polly Pocket doll and a few books that we brought with us from the States. We hadn't been in Haiti much more than a month, but Isabel's face lit up as she opened these gifts that brought with them a familiar feeling of the comforts of home. It was a great moment.

We finished the day with cake and singing for Isabel back on campus. As I lay down that night, I was so thankful to Pastor for making the hike happen. I was thankful for my daughter who came into the world eight years prior. And I was thankful to God for such a great experience. But in the back of my mind, as sleep began to come, I was still thinking about Clement and his neighbors.

Lost in Translation

It took us a couple of weeks, but we finally tracked down some tarps. Jay Shultz and I loaded them up in Pastor's old Toyota and slowly made our way back up the mountain. We took Clerice, one of our Haitian staff, along with us to serve as our interpreter. No sooner did we get going when we were stopped at a police checkpoint.

Normally they see us *blans*, in the truck and they simply wave us along, at least that had been my experience thus far. But this time was different. "Can I see your license?" the officer asked me in Creole, or so I assumed. Clerice had gone strangely silent.

"I'm from Chambrun, I'm from Chambrun," I responded in English. I had forgotten my license back at our tent, so I began to insist louder, "I'm from Chambrun…you know, Pastor Pierre? Nehemiah?" I pointed to the NVM insignia on my shirt as evidence, which apparently meant nothing to the policeman.

"*Pale Angle?*" the officer turned to Clerice and asked.

"No," Clerice responded, shrugging his shoulders. Brilliant, I thought. Way to come through when we need you, Clerice. Not only was he not translating for us, but he was lying to this Haitian cop.

The officer inspected our truck, looking around to make sure we weren't transporting anything illegal. He walked around the front of the truck to ensure our sticker on the passenger side windshield was up-to-date. "Dumb Americans…you think you can just come in here and drive around with no license," the officer muttered under his breath. Clerice gave us this translation after the fact.

He finally waved us on, not wanting to have to deal with us any longer. "*Ale!*" he waved. That's all we needed to hear.

I put the truck back into first gear and said a quick prayer. "Come on, truck. Don't fail me now." As I prayed this, the old Toyota lurched loudly into first gear, and we were on our way.

Winding back towards Clement's house, Jay laughed, looking at Clerice. "Oh, so you don't speak English now?"

Clerice responded with his wide smile, "If I told him I spoke English, we would have been there a whole lot longer. They would have asked us all sorts of questions, and we would have ended up at the same place any way." Fair or not, there are times when being a *blan* has its advantages in Haiti.

Tarp Delivery

We made it to Clement's *joupa*. I parked in the wrong spot, and we had to all jump over a ditch—me favoring a pulled hamstring, and Jay with his notoriously bad back. We heaved our failing bodies across this ravine and came up hobbling pathetically. Clerice deftly bounded up the trail leaving us behind, the heavy tarps safely on his head. An outside observer would have laughed at these two hobbling *blans* being left behind by the young Haitian with heavy tarps on his head.

Everyone in Clement's "neighborhood" was thrilled to receive the tarps. Actually, it was the old sidewall of a tent that used to serve as the church. It was nice and thick, and one of Clement's neighbors cut the tarp into four equal pieces to distribute them over the homes. It appeared we brought just the right amount for all four homes. A few of the children living in the houses walked with us back to the truck, following us and pretending we were human jungle gyms. Anyone who has been on a trip to the third world and does not know the local language can identify with this phenomenon. All you're seemingly good for is for kids to use you as living playground equipment. This was especially unpleasant for Jay and I, who had just proven we were anything but gymnasts. There were giant thorn bushes all over the ground, and we hobbled carefully down the mountain to avoid them. Clement's young daughter held my hand and walked with us barefoot. As we walked, she stepped directly on a thorn bush and kept right on walking. She didn't flinch..

"Jay, did you see that?" I asked.

"Yeah, I saw it," he responded. "This girl has tough feet."

A Gift Exchange

Clement has been near to my heart ever since that day. We delivered the tarp on Thursday, and on Saturday, one of the organizations who was doing a major building project at NVM bought bacon and eggs and prepared bacon, egg, and cheese omelets that would make Denny's jealous. They made this special treat for their team and NVM's staff. I'll never forget Clement walking in that morning. He came in to fill up his cooler with ice and water and there I was, a steaming omelet in front of me, and Clement had his eye on it. I know how Clement lives. No way has he ever eaten what sat right in front of me. And I know Clement could see what we were all enjoying. I was flooded with emotion.

Why am I sitting here eating this and Clement is not? Clement works from 6:00 in the morning until 6:00 in the evening for about $2.00 a day, and that is a fair wage in this context. How can I eat this with all these people when he is only given lunch? What is the difference between Clement and I other than I was born in the USA and have had lots of opportunities when Clement was born in rural Haiti?

It was painful eating my breakfast that morning. I instantly lost my appetite, but heard a small reminder in my head from Pastor Pierre that individuals that come on teams need to make sure they eat while here, even as they wrestle with what they experience. So I forced it down.

I also committed to serving Clement anyway that I was able. A simple way became the act of filling his ice bucket and water bottle anytime he was in the cafeteria the same time I was there. Sitota became my best helper in this small act of service. I know I am doing many other things that indirectly help Clement, but this was one small tangible way I might serve this gentle man.

About a month later, we built a guard shack for the security guards, with Clement in mind. When the sun is burning hot, which it often is in Haiti, or the rain is coming down in waves, the guards need a place to find shelter. We built an eight-foot by four-foot wood structure with two windows that you can fold up or down. The shack has a nice blue and white coat of paint on it and a sloped roof. When we were building it, Clement stood by and commented, "This is nicer than my house." Having been there myself, I knew he was speaking the truth.

One day shortly after the shack was completed, I was leaving campus in our white truck when I noticed Clement had brought his family to see it. They were so taken by it that I thought they were going to move in.

It says in James: "Has not God chosen those who are poor in the eyes of the world to be rich in faith and to inherit the kingdom he promised those who love him?" The poor indeed are rich in faith, and I have received some unbelievable gifts from Clement and the overflow of his heart. When we danced outside his house after praying for him, I knew I had been given a gift. When his daughter escorted me down the mountain, I knew I had received another gift. Every time I drive in and out of campus and see his deferential bow and wave, I know I am receiving a gift. Clement's faith and joyful spirit are downright infectious, and he offers them freely.

I have been working long enough with teams to know that many of them come with their own strong agendas, determined to help. They all have the purest motives, and it is all good. But more often than not, when the end of a team's time comes, I will hear the comment "I feel like I received so much more than I gave." This certainly characterizes how I feel about my relationship with Clement.

Clement received some valuable gifts from my team and me. We gave him a tarp to keep the rain outside his house. We gave him a good job and built a guard shack for him to shelter him during the day. Even the act of filling up his ice bucket is a gift that gives him dignity and shows Clement that we value him. In spite of all this, I find myself echoing the thoughts of the teams who come serve: I receive indescribably more than I give in knowing Clement.

5 THE MAN WITH NO FACE

"For our battle is not against flesh and blood but against the powers and
principalities of this world."
- Ephesians 6:12

Ephesians 6:12 is tough to interpret, but the gist of it for me is that our struggles in life are largely not against the people we run into—it's not against flesh and blood. There are spiritual forces at work taking advantage of every opportunity to ruin our lives—especially if we follow Christ.

Into the Ditch

We were sitting in the dining hall one night eating dinner with a large team of at least forty people, along with most of our Haitian staff. Suddenly, Pastor Pierre comes running through the doorway, and yells, "Kacie, Aubree, I need you, now!" By the look of his face and the sound of his voice, this was serious.

I had literally my first bite of dinner in my mouth at this point. I remember thinking this is the first time I have sat down in twelve hours. Oh well, T.I.H...This is Haiti. The American staff started saying this to each other after seeing *Blood Diamond*, where Leonardo DiCaprio's character says "T.I.A."(This is Africa) anytime things go completely wrong in a way that could only happen in Africa. In Haiti, this phrase is not only the same, but, I would wager, even more applicable because there is always something happening that would seem out of the realm of possibility or beyond what is rational back in the States. If I had known what was going on outside, I probably would not have had such a self-centered reaction.

I abandoned dinner, running outside just in time to see Kacie and Aubree getting on the back of a motorcycle and riding to the other side of campus. I half-jogged over to one of NVM's trucks. At this point, I had already driven one person to the hospital in it, and I knew this was pretty much the only practical skill I had to offer in Haiti. I headed to the far side of campus, where the entrance gate was located. Someone was hurt. I could tell that much. I turned the truck lights on to shine some light on what was happening.

When I got there, I could see Pastor's truck nose-down in a ditch. For the life of me, I couldn't figure out how it got there. There is a gate at the entrance and a fence that extends about ten yards. Where the fence ends, there is a little bit of a dirt ridge the truck would have to go over before it dropped into the ditch. There were several kids lying in the ditch, completely covered in mud. One boy in particular was not moving. This is where Kacie and Aubree rushed off to. It looked like we might already be too late. I started to pray from behind the windshield of the truck.

We focused our attention on this boy, whose name I later learned is Herbie. He didn't appear to be breathing at first, but upon further inspection, Kacie and Aubree found that Herbie was still alive, but hurt badly.

It was chaos—completely crazy. Kids covered head to toe in mud, adults pulling them out apparently suffering from shock, clearly stunned, a truck that somehow is nose first in a ditch and one boy who needs serious medical attention. Pastor was beside himself—absolutely distraught.

Pastor had already pulled the injured boy out of the mud, so we carefully put him on a board and carried him to the clinic, fearing a back or neck injury. By this time, it was pitch black outside—the clinic long closed and locked for the night. Inside the clinic, Kacie and Aubree began to treat Herbie. He had a cut under his nose that split his lip and a bigger one on his forehead. His forehead had already begun to swell. Herbie's mother came in, and she immediately collapsed on the floor, crying uncontrollably at the sight of her badly injured son. At this point, our nurses had determined that Herbie's injuries weren't critical, but that he still needed to go to the hospital to get treatment and ensure his head and internal organs were not damaged.

Herbie was loaded back onto the board and into the back of the truck. I drove it to Bernard Meivs Hosptial, also known to us as Miami-Dade Hospital, in Port-au-Prince. We were in a hurry, but Haitian traffic did not comply. The sooner we got this boy to the hospital, the better, in my mind. I found myself turning two lane roads into three, aggressively trying to push my way through traffic. This would be the first time eleven-year-old Herbie was to ever leave his hometown of Chambrun.

When we got to the hospital, the doctors and nurses thought Herbie needed some stitches, but that his injury was not anything serious. "You need to look at his head again," Kacie and Aubree insisted. "He may have a skull fracture." It took quite a few suggestions, but their persistence paid off. The doctors decided to give Herbie an x-ray and, after doing so, they found that he did, in fact, have a skull fracture. They did not need to do surgery right away, but they did not rule it out, so Herbie needed to stay the night to see if the swelling increased. He received several stitches on his head and many more under his nose and inside his lip. Herbie stayed overnight at the hospital and fortunately showed no signs of worsening. I drove him home the next day when he was released.

Herbie is a beautiful young man. We consider it miraculous that he did not suffer more than he did. The stiches eventually came out, and the scars are minimal. He is back in school, a happy kid, playing with the others in the village and for all intents and purposes, back to normal life. Well, except for being a local celebrity among the other inquisitive kids who have never been out of Chambrun.

Rewind

Later on, Pastor Pierre told us the story.

Several of the children came up to Pastor, saying, "You're always too busy for us. Why do you never play with us anymore?"

So he replied with a playful smile, "Get in the truck."

The kids hopped in the back of the truck with eager anticipation. Pastor is always great with the kids and would never do anything to intentionally put them in danger. In fact, a serious accident could put him and NVM in danger of shutting down completely. As I mentioned previously, Pastor is extremely safety-conscious and would never knowingly put someone in harm's way.

Pastor began to drive the kids around, doing slow doughnuts in the field. The kids were all giddy with laughter. He got out of the truck after putting it in neutral—he swears to this—allowing the truck to roll a little bit. The truck was rolling along and Pastor could easily get back in, but to the kids, it created that small sense of thrill and nervousness, the kind my three-year-old gets when I toss him into the stratosphere, only to safely catch him upon his descent to earth. He was in complete control of the situation, or so it seemed.

As Pastor Pierre walked alongside the slow rolling truck, the truck began to speed up. Before he knew it, the truck started to get away from him. It began to go fast enough that he couldn't catch up to it. The kids all saw the look on Pastor's face. They started to yell, "Stop, truck!"

The game was turning into a nightmare.

The truck slipped between a parked box truck and a fence, threading the needle, climbing up an embankment. It navigated up a sharp incline, gaining speed the whole time, and careened all the way down into the ditch, which is where we eventually found the kids laying in the mud, stunned, scared and filthy.

Making Sense Out of Things

I went to the field the next day. The route this truck took seemed highly unlikely, and I wanted to conduct my own test. I took a truck of the same make and model out to see if it would behave in the same way the other truck did. I put the truck in first gear and let the clutch out. The truck would quickly stall just creeping along the earth. There was no way it would climb an incline. I looked at where Pastor started and took note of the gap between the fence and box truck. Again—this doesn't add up, I thought to myself. How did the truck steer for this narrow gap that allowed access to the ditch?

It makes no sense that Pastor's truck ended up in the ditch—none whatsoever. In addition to the unlikely increase in speed at the incline, the truck's route is impossible. The width of where the truck had to navigate was maybe one and a half times the width of the truck. It had to make a series of subtle turns to miss running into objects like the fence and parked box truck. For it to go straight through that course, someone had to be driving it. The circumstances of the whole situation made no sense. I went back, scratching my head in disbelief.

How on earth did this happen?

Pastor took it hard. It was the most shaken I had seen him up to this point in my year. A child got badly hurt while on his watch, and the story itself doesn't quite line up. Herbie could have easily died, and NVM would have been shut down for endangering the lives of the children it serves. Pastor even started mouth-to-mouth on Herbie because he thought that Herbie had already stopped breathing. We're not sure if Herbie, in fact, had stopped breathing, or if Pastor was simply in shock and couldn't sense a pulse in Herbie's mud-covered body.

But then things got weird. One of the children in the back of the truck approached Pastor Pierre with an eerie account. He told Pastor that "a man with no face" got behind the wheel and drove the truck into the ditch.

Spiritual and Cultural Differences

Sometimes Haitians will retell a story in different ways. I am not sure if their method of storytelling is strictly a cultural way of recounting events, or if their stories actually happen literally as they are telling it. I have learned many Haitian proverbs from Jay Shultz as he has taken it upon himself to learn many of the obscure ones in Creole to impress the Haitians we work with. These proverbs have a way of describing reality for Haitian culture.

Was "a man with no face" some kind of metaphor or Haitian idiom?

At the same time, Haiti is a place where people believe in spiritual realities differently than we do in the U.S. For example, they believe in zombies—not like Night of the Living Dead, but many Haitians will tell you that they have been to a loved one's funeral and seen them walking around in the market the next day. There is a very famous and well-documented account of a young girl who was back among the living a week after she was buried. Pastor Pierre knows the pastor who presided over her funeral. Knowing this context, it was very difficult for me to know what this phrase meant.

Another cultural difference is that, in the States, we would immediately ask the question: who is to blame? In the case of this accident, fingers would start to point at Pastor. But this isn't how Haiti works. When our Haitian housekeeper dropped one of our glasses, and it broke into hundreds of tiny shards, she told us "The glass broke." Not, "I broke the glass" or "I dropped the glass", but "the glass broke."

I realized my mind thinks in a very American way: this happened. It's someone's fault. This kid almost died...who is to blame? None of these questions or problems popped into anyone else's head (among the Haitians). This was strictly an American way of thinking, to establish fault. To the Haitians, it was a given that this event happened, but they were less concerned with how. This just happened.

Three Options

When the child came to Pastor Pierre and said that a man with no face got in the truck and drove it, this was the closest anyone came to explaining what happened or who was at fault. In my mind, one of three things is possible.

First of all, Pastor Pierre could have used the man with no face as a way to cover up his own fault. As I write this last sentence, I wanted to take this first option completely out of the story. This goes so strongly against everything I have experienced with Pastor Pierre that it is an insult to think my mind would even conjure up the possibility. Would he have knowingly put himself, the children, and his entire ministry (which is his life) at jeopardy, and when something bad happened, cover it up with a lie from a child? Impossible. I repent of my terrible thoughts.

Secondly, only one of the kids came up and gave this explanation. It could have been his imagination running wild in an attempt to account for what happened. Maybe he dreamed it up. This could be the case, but it does not account for how the truck made its way through an obstacle course, accelerated up a hill with no one in it, and ended up nose-first in a ditch. Even if Pastor had left the truck in first gear (which he didn't), it would have needed to accelerate in order to go up the hill or stall out. The truck didn't drive itself. Yet in the world I know, faceless men don't exist.

The third explanation is simple, albeit unbelievable to my understanding of what is possible up to this point in life: a man with no face drove the truck into the ditch. It may or may not have been a literal, physical person, but nothing else explains how the truck navigated around objects, through a tight space, accelerated up a hill, and dove into the ditch. Its intent was evil and malicious. Its aim was to injure these children. Its objective was to damage Pastor Pierre's reputation. Its goal was to kill Herbie or one of the other children.

How in the world can I explain this?

Targets on Our Back

This event is still not clearly understood or explained, but when I read the Bible, I get a sense that there is much more going on than what my whitewashed, suburban world would lead me to believe. In 1 Peter 5 it says, "Be alert and of sober mind. Your enemy the devil prowls around like a roaring lion looking for someone to devour." We have an enemy that will kill children.

It is a miracle that Herbie wasn't more seriously hurt than he was. When we first found him, things looked grim. He fractured his skull and received stitches in two places. Head injuries usually don't heal so quickly and completely. Today, Herbie is a happy, good-looking kid with a joyful spirit. He is back living in a mud home with his mother and four siblings.

I realize this story is bizarre. Part of me hesitates in telling it because of my own lack of understanding. There was so much more going on in the realm of what is unseen than what I can explain. Part of me even hesitates to tell it because I don't think people will believe it. Yet, within the community of Haitians where I live, they easily accept a story of a man with no face. In my Western, rational mindset, I struggle to believe it. But I do believe this is what happened.

Ignorance vs. Vigilance

We find it easier to live life as if Peter's warnings in 1 Peter 5 weren't true. We act like if we don't believe it, it isn't true. C.S. Lewis' *Screwtape Letters* is a satirical novel with a series of letters back and forth between a senior demon and his nephew, Wormwood. In the preface, Lewis writes:

There are two equal and opposite errors into which our race can fall about the devils. One is to disbelieve in their existence. The other is to believe, and to feel an excessive and unhealthy interest in them. They themselves are equally pleased by both errors and hail a materialist or a magician with the same delight. (Lewis)

In Haiti there is not only an assumption of the spiritual world, but also proof of it. I'm not sure if the man with no face was a way to make sense out of what happened or if it was literally a spiritual being taking on a physical form and driving a truck into a ditch. In either case, I am confident that there is so much more going on than what my five senses tell me: that is for sure. Scripture tells us this, and my experience confirms it. The good work we are trying to do is not "cool" with everybody.

There is a reality to the scripture in 1 Peter at work in this story. Even if this man with no face didn't manifest literally, I believe Satan showed up in some way with the intent to destroy all the good work Pastor Pierre and countless others have been building through the ministry of NVM. We have an enemy whose goal is to ruin our personal lives, as well as all the work God has been doing through us. Some would call this work our ministry. He wants to wreak havoc on our ministry, wrecking the kingdom-building work of every Christ follower. If you follow Christ, this applies to you. If you follow Christ, Satan is gunning for you. As Peter advises, be alert!

How those kids ended up in the ditch makes absolutely no sense to me. How a kid who had a fractured skull and all those stitches turned out so healthy doesn't make a whole lot of sense either. All I know is that while there are forces trying to trip us up at every turn, there's a much stronger Force fighting on our behalf.

"You, dear children, are from God and have overcome them, because the one who is in you is greater than the one who is in the world." 1 John 4:4.

6 VISIONS AND DREAMS

"And afterward, I will pour out my Spirit on all people. Your sons and daughters will prophesy, your old men will dream dreams, your young men will see visions. Even on my servants, both men and women, I will pour out my Spirit in those days."
- Joel 2:28-29

I have always liked this passage in Joel. It speaks of a time when God will pour himself out into his people. I remember a New Testament professor pointing out in the Gospel of Luke the partial fulfillment of this passage. You can read the story in Luke 2:25-38. Jesus is taken to be presented in the temple, and a man named Simeon and a woman named Anna each prophesy and tell Mary and Joseph about their child Jesus. It is truly a fascinating story—rather bizarre really—and a literal fulfillment of this passage in Joel.

This passage is also directly quoted one time in the New Testament. In Acts 2, after the crowds all think the disciples are drunk because of the way they were acting—overcome by the Holy Spirit—Peter stands up and quotes this verse. He defends the disciples, saying they aren't drunk, but full of the Spirit of Jesus, who they put to death. Apparently his talk had quite an impact because it says that 3000 came to faith in Jesus when Peter quit talking.

Never did I think I would actually see this verse in Joel come to be before my own eyes.

Twins

It was mid-February and a medical team was on campus along with Dr. Bill Burgess, a dentist who has been coming to Haiti and NVM for years. He brought with him two hygienists who would be assisting him, and they brought their husbands to help in any way they could. One of the couples, Jerry and Stephanie, were in Haiti for the first time.

Jerry and Stephanie have a blended family back home. I don't remember how many children they each have with a previous spouse, but I remember Jerry's son was an exceptional soccer player, one of the best fifty in the country for his age. I love soccer and my ears perked up when he was talking about his son and his passion for soccer. They had some other older children as well, but I honestly couldn't remember them all. I got the sense that they had a large family and a real heart for children.

We took them down to the children's home where we currently have nine children under our care. The kids in the home are used to groups coming to visit them and are so gracious to invite our many friends into their home and into their lives. Often a soccer game or some other fun activity will form.

On this particular day, Jerry and Stephanie were visiting the home. As Jerry came in, one of our little boys, we will call him Nu-Nu (not his real name) immediately ran into Jerry's arms and would not part with him. They laughed and played together for the better part of the afternoon. Around the side of the home, Stephanie instantly bonded with another little boy name Lei-Lei (also not his real name). Lei Lei came right up to her and never left her side the entire time she was at the home. Both of them fell instantly in love with their respective little boys.

As they got back to campus, they were joking about adopting each of their little boys. "But how would we decide which one?" they seemed to be asking one another. One of our staff calmly pointed out, "You do know they are twins, right?" I wish I could show you the look on their faces when they discovered they were twins. It was priceless...a mix of shock, disbelief, astonishment...maybe breathless captures it. I was about to learn the back story that caused such a highly emotional reaction.

The Prayers of a Six-year Old

Some weeks before Jerry and Stephanie boarded the plane to come to Haiti, they started preparing their youngest son for their absence. They let him know that they were going to help the people of Haiti. They began to teach him of the work NVM is doing and the little kids that need help, kids just like him. Very quickly the little boy started to say that his Mommy (Stephanie) was going to come home with two six-year old twin boys in her belly. Jerry and Stephanie both laughed when they first heard this, having no idea where he got the idea. It started one night when they put him to bed.

The next night at the dinner table, the tradition is to let their son pray before the meal. This night he prayed again that Mom and Dad would bring home twin six-year old brothers from Haiti. He dropped the "in Mommy's belly part." I think Stephanie may have communicated in no uncertain terms that she would not be bringing home any babies in her belly. Six-year old brothers would be the same age as their son and certainly provide some outstanding playmates.

The next night rolled around and the same thing happened. Prayers to God that Mom and Dad would bring home twin six-year old boys from Haiti. And night after night, without fail, their little boy would pray before dinner for two twin six-year old brothers to come home from Haiti. Every night, all the way up until they left.

Jerry and Stephanie always laughed at their son, and his prayer became a part of the evening routine. Never really sure where the idea came from, thinking he must have gotten in his head the idea of brothers or something from a friend at school, but always laughing and joking around with him each night as he would pray.

Nu-Nu and Lei-Lei's age of course? Six years old.

When they realized that they had just met six-year-old twin boys, they immediately remembered the weeks of their own son praying that they would come home with brothers. This was just way too weird for Jerry and Stephanie. Frankly, for me as I was listening to this story, it was weird.

Rest of the Week

Jerry and Stephanie spent as much time as they were able with Nu-Nu and Lei-Lei the rest of the week. They learned that their parents had both passed away. Their mother apparently had died in childbirth, and the father passed away in the earthquake. They were left in the care of an uncle who could not care for them, and so they were signed over into the care of NVM's children's home. Nu-Nu and Lei-Lei are true orphans, in part from the devastating earthquake.

I can still remember the first time I met these boys. They left a strong impression on me. I was at church in July 2010 when we were still meeting under the big circus tent. The boys each had on sport coats and were the sharpest looking kids in the place. They were somewhat quiet and reserved, but connected to one another as only twins can. I have seen other teams come and go with visits to the children's home, and Nu-Nu and Lei-Lei had not taken to anyone else quite like they took to Jerry and Stephanie. Jerry and Stephanie had a picture of themselves printed off somehow, and they left it with the boys to hang on the wall next to their bed so as to remember them.

Unfinished

Before they left, Jerry and Stephanie sat down with Pastor to inquire about adopting Nu-Nu and Lei-Lei. Although adoption is not the goal with the children in our children's home, under special circumstances we will allow someone to pursue it. Pastor had Gestin talk to the boy's uncle and found out he would sign the necessary paperwork to adopt the boys. It would be possible for Jerry and Stephanie to bring the boys into their family.

Stephanie is a dental hygienist, and Jerry was in between jobs at the time. They were going to go home and pray about what they should do. At the time of writing this, they had inquired once about coming to live for a year down here and working in the soon-to-be-opened children's homes. But nothing concrete has developed…yet.

I have heard Pastor quote many times this year a passage from Philippians 1:

"I thank my God every time I remember you. In all my prayers for all of you, I always pray with joy because of your partnership in the gospel from the first day until now, being confident of this, that he who began a good work in you will carry it on to completion until the day of Christ Jesus."

Paul was confident that when God starts a work, He is faithful to complete it. I think much of our challenge in life as followers of Jesus is to try and cooperate and stay out of the way of what God has planned. He is faithful. I still don't know what this means for Jerry and Stephanie, or for Nu-Nu and Lei-Lei, but I am amazed at the first part of this story and look forward to how it will be completed. And I wonder how the conversation went with their son who faithfully prayed every night prior to their trip?

7 AN UNFORGETTABLE EASTER

On one occasion an expert in the law stood up to test Jesus. "Teacher," he asked, "what must I do to inherit eternal life?" "What is written in the Law?" he replied. "How do you read it?" He answered: "'Love the Lord your God with all your heart and with all your soul and with all your strength and with all your mind'; and, 'Love your neighbor as yourself.'" "You have answered correctly," Jesus replied. "Do this and you will live." But he wanted to justify himself, so he asked Jesus, "And who is my neighbor?" In reply Jesus said: "A man was going down from Jerusalem to Jericho, when he fell into the hands of robbers. They stripped him of his clothes, beat him and went away, leaving him half dead. A priest happened to be going down the same road, and when he saw the man, he passed by on the other side. So too, a Levite, when he came to the place and saw him, passed by on the other side. But a Samaritan, as he traveled, came where the man was; and when he saw him, he took pity on him. He went to him and bandaged his wounds, pouring on oil and wine. Then he put the man on his own donkey, took him to an inn and took care of him. The next day he took out two silver coins and gave them to the innkeeper. 'Look after him,' he said, 'and when I return, I will reimburse you for any extra expense you may have.' "Which of these three do you think was a neighbor to the man who fell into the hands of robbers?" The expert in the law replied, "The one who had mercy on him." Jesus told him, "Go and do likewise."
-Luke 10:25-37

An Attempt at Familiarity

I woke up with Sitota around 6:00 a.m. Easter morning. I had no idea why I was up so early, but we quietly got dressed and headed to the church for the morning Easter service, which was scheduled to begin at 6. When we got there at 6:10, there were about ten other people there. There is no such thing as "on time" here in Haiti. it's more like "Haiti time" (which, by the way, is strikingly similar to "college time"). T.I.H. Sitota and I walked back to get breakfast. The night before I had hidden Easter baskets for the kids, which of course needed to be searched for and thoroughly inspected upon discovery. By the time the rest of the family woke up, got dressed, ate breakfast, found their Easter baskets, and managed to get back to church, the service was half over. Apparently, the music started around 6:30, and the actual Easter church service started closer to 7.

Shortly after lunch, the generator on campus died. Without the generator running, we do not have power and water on the campus. We were preparing a big Easter meal and needed these things to pull it off. After many starts and stops, we discovered that some dirty fuel had clogged the fuel filter. After it was removed, cleaned, and put back on, we started it up and it seemed to be running well again. Pastor Pierre left campus telling me he was going to find a new filter for the generator. Because of the delay while the generator was off, our turkey feast was pushed back closer to 6:00 p.m. instead of the planned time of 2:00 p.m. In the meantime, we had an Easter egg hunt with the Schultz kids in the men's bathhouse, of all places. This was the best, most available place to hide 41 eggs, where it wasn't too hot, and they could be easily found.

Interruption

After our Easter egg hunt, I received a call from Pastor Pierre. The local chief at the new police station up the road had called him to see if one of our nurses could come set a man's foot. An accident just occurred, and someone needed immediate attention. They told us we didn't have to take him to the hospital, but simply triage and then we would be back to the Easter festivities. No problem. Our days seemed to be filled mostly with interruptions like this. This seemed like just one more in a string of many.

So I went looking for Aubree and Kacie with a moderate sense of urgency. I didn't run to find them—it was more of a power mall-walk speed. I found them in their tent playing with baby Rosemelie from the village. Rosemelie is a very special girl to NVM and our nurses, having been literally saved from death many times by their intervention and care. Kacie decided to stay behind since we were only going to "set a foot," and there was nowhere to leave baby Rose. Aubree could handle some basic first aid on her own anyway.

Aubree and I made our way to the clinic to put together some supplies.

"Hey Aubree," I said, "You may want to grab some gloves. I'm not sure what condition this guy is in. Pastor said they asked us to set his foot before they took him to the hospital."

"That's true," she replied, grabbing a few more supplies. We hopped in the truck and sped down the road towards the police station.

As we were headed off campus, I grabbed Clerice, our "mute" translator. Clerice is extremely generous, a solid translator, has a deep love for his people, and possesses a strong desire to go to the U.S. to get an education so that he can come back and serve the people of Haiti. Clerice has vision, and he gets the vision of NVM. If he stays true to what God has put in his heart, he will be one of the people who make a long-term difference. Clerice, Aubree and I all loaded up and sped off down the road to the police station.

We arrived at the police station in no more than five minutes. Our truck has an NVM magnet on the driver's side door that indicates our association with NVM. I saw the three officers look at me oddly, move their eyes to the door, make the connection, and quickly point up the road. The accident had happened maybe a hundred yards further up the road.

High Stakes Triage

Pulling up to the scene, I saw a dump truck off in the brush a few hundred feet away, with a downed power line pole in its wake. The next thing I spotted was a man lying in the ditch, just off the side of the road on my left.

I slowly pulled past the police truck parked next to him and was bringing our truck to a stop when I noticed his foot. It reminded me of one of my daughters' dolls when it has its leg twisted the wrong way—this man's leg was pointing in the wrong direction.

My mind started to race. This guy was either standing on the side of the road or he was sitting on top of the dump truck when the accident happened; I never did get the story straight. As I brought our pick-up to a stop, I kept thinking this guy's leg looks severed.

At this point, Aubree sprang into action. It's an amazing thing to watch a medical professional get to work doing what they are trained to do. She quickly jumped out of the truck and could tell this man was not doing well. Shock was setting in, and he wasn't making any sense. Aubree needed something to cut the loose pants from his leg so she could get a better look at the injury. One of the onlookers had a dull machete in his possession. We went to work cutting the pant leg off with the machete. As we did this, Aubree discovered that his leg was severed in two places—one near the top of his leg and another near the bottom. It appeared that his skin was the only thing holding it in place.

"Aaron!" Aubree ordered with a sense of urgency, "We need to get him to the nearest hospital—fast!"

There was already blood soaking into the dry Haitian dirt in the entire area. How long has he been lying here? Why was this police officer just standing around doing nothing? Is he in shock as well?

I shook off my thoughts and replied to Aubree, "Do we need a tourniquet?"

"Yes."

I looked around. "Who has a belt?"

I didn't have one. Neither did Clerice. The onlooker who had loaned us his machete had one. I gestured to him to give us his belt. "Clerice, tell him we will get him another one!" The man hesitated to take off his belt, but, reluctantly, he handed it over.

Aubree fastened a tourniquet high up on his leg.

"We need to move him. He's losing more blood every second."

My gaze quickly shot over to the police officer. Which truck are we taking him in? He seemed to be looking to me for the answer. The whole time Clerice was having conversations with the onlookers in Creole. My Creole is so basic, and they were talking so quickly I couldn't follow. But I trusted Clerice completely. He didn't have any confidence about us taking the man in our truck. I looked over at Aubree. She seemed to read my mind.

"Aaron, this is an emergency!"

"Right…we don't really have a choice. Let's load him up right now. We need to get him to the hospital."

Aubree, Clerice and I loaded him into the back of the truck as quickly and carefully as we could. I was thankful that I was lifting his still intact leg as we loaded him.

"Clerice, tell the officer we will follow him to the hospital. He can lead the way."

We followed the police truck gingerly back down to the police station. I looked in the rearview mirror and saw Aubree in the bed of our truck with the injured guy. I knew from prior hospital runs (this was now my third) that Aubree gets a little nervous with my style of driving through Port-au-Prince traffic.

"Clerice, I need you to get in the back and help Aubree."

As we pulled up to the police station, the officer in the truck ahead of us was having a conversation while Clerice hopped in the back of our truck.

Finally after a little urging, the officer pulled out with us trailing behind him. I knew it was about sixteen miles to the airport, and hopefully we were going somewhere nearby. I only knew Miami-Dade hospital, and they were saying something about Delmas 21. On a Sunday afternoon, we should be able to get there pretty quickly, especially behind a police truck.

Except we weren't. We were moving so slowly. Why don't we get moving?

As I shifted into third gear, the police truck suddenly dropped into a lower gear, his tires screeching. I slammed on the brakes, swerving to the left side of the road, and came within inches of smashing into the back of him. I checked my mirror, thankful that I hadn't thrown Clerice or Aubree out of the truck. I pulled up next to him and could tell by his face that he was full of fear. He didn't know how to operate the truck's manual transmission.

I glanced in the rearview mirror again. At this point, every second mattered.

If we leave him, then what? I wasn't confident in this police officer, but I also didn't really know where we were going, either.

I decided to leave him behind.

Suddenly a second police truck drove by. This one was from Meyer, which was the next small town up the road. He turned the lights on, blared the sirens, and started really moving. This is more like it.

Now I was smashing the accelerator, struggling to keep up with this lead-footed police officer. I was afraid of going too fast with the patient and two caretakers on the back of our truck. As we rounded the small bend into Meyer, this policeman abruptly pulled over. I pulled up next to him, urging him (in English, which was not helpful) to take us to the hospital as quickly as possible. Clerice was yelling from the back, probably telling him the same things I was saying.

"We will follow you! Take us to the hospital…you lead, we will follow!"

"No! No!" was his only reply.

The message was clear. This policeman was not leaving his post. We were on our own.

Taking Matters Into Our Own Hands

Aubree yelled from the back: "Let's just go to Miami-Dade!"

"Okay, hang on!"

A few vivid images stuck with me from the drive. We had a number of close calls as I made a two-lane road three lanes. We came across an angry tap-tap driver who called me a dog when I quickly exited the roundabout the wrong way in front of him, jumping the curb. Clerice was nice enough to defend my driving tactics with a shout of "pig!" in Creole from the back of the truck. And I remember the feeling of urgency at every moment as we made our way into the city.

Thankfully, we got to Miami-Dade quickly, and my frantic driving didn't hurt anyone. We pulled up to the hospital and handed our patient off to the more than capable staff. We borrowed some scrubs so Aubree could take a quick shower and change out of her blood-soaked clothes, and then we started back home.

As we left, there was good news, and there was bad news. The good news: we probably saved the guy's life. The bad news: he lost a lot of blood, and the orthopedic doctor who was headed to surgery didn't think he was going to be able to save the guy's leg. As far as Clerice, Aubree and I were concerned, we stopped and bought some Coke and Tampico, our favorite

Haitian beverages, for the drive home. After this Easter experience, I thought the least I could do was spring for drinks to say thanks for an otherwise thankless job well done.

It was one week later, on a Sunday, when an officer from the post that originally asked us to help stopped by our campus. He off-handedly mentioned to Aubree that the man we tried to help ended up dying. This news landed like a ton of bricks on all of our hearts. The man died on Easter, the day Christians celebrate that death is overcome!

Questions

I know the point of the Good Samaritan story Jesus told was to show how we are to act towards one another. We should act as if everyone is our neighbor. And by asking the question, "What happens if you return and find out the man has died?," I am asking an entirely different question than the one posed to Jesus. But it is the question I am asking, and with plenty of emotion behind it, on several levels.

On one level I am processing my personal emotions. What was up with all the unhelpful people we encountered? There were the police officers...some that seemed to not want to be involved, some that would not (or could not?) leave their jurisdiction and the guy that could not drive a stick shift. There was the man on the side of the road that was just short of unwilling to part with his belt. And what about the driver of the dump truck? How did the truck go flying off the road, on a slight uphill? Is this the result of yet another poorly maintained vehicle? And then what do I do with the knowledge that he died? What if I had driven faster...would it have mattered? What if I had run instead of walked around campus? I don't think I could have driven any faster. And plus, I didn't even know this guy. I still do not even know his name, and yet his death weighs heavy.

Then there is another level of questions, the level of systemic injustice Haiti has suffered for centuries from corrupt political leadership. After over 200 years of independence, Haiti still lacks the basic infrastructure that governments are supposed to help provide. The police are untrained, the roads are terrible, there is a tremendous lack of access to hospitals and health care facilities, all factors that we encountered. We were called because of the relationship Pastor has with the local chief. What would have happened if the chief didn't call us...I suppose he would have died on the road? And where does the mindset come from that fears the risk of liability over trying to do good (in this case, rush a man to the hospital and try and save his life).

And perhaps on a third level, I am asking a question about justice in general. Why do some people live and some people die in what seems like very random ways? I suppose anyone who has been to war and had their brother next to them killed in the heat of battle while they lived has asked some version of this question. Why? Why are some born in Haiti while I was born in suburban USA? Is justice only achieved after death in eternity? I am bound by my limited perspective. Some questions are asked for the sake of asking them, not necessarily to get a clear answer.

These questions still plague my thoughts, but in the specific moment of trying to help this man, it was clear what needed to be done, and we acted accordingly. It was clear in the parable of the good Samaritan who acted as neighbor. Jesus told the story in such a way that it was painfully obvious.

I told Pastor later that he ruined my Easter. But I followed that with the clear statement: If the police call again, please tell them we will try to help. We will try and do the same thing next time.

8 JUNE 15, 2011

So, if you think you are standing firm, be careful that you don't fall! No temptation has seized you except what is common to man. And God is faithful; he will not let you be tempted beyond what you can bear. But when you are tempted, he will also provide a way out so that you can stand up under it.
-1 Corinthians 10:12-13

Christians often quote this verse as an encouragement to others when they are overwhelmed by their circumstances. It usually sounds like some version of "God will not give you more than you can handle." I think it is intended as a pick-me up, an encouragement that you can do this, whatever "this" may be, if you just hang in there. God is faithful to see you through.

Sometimes I want to punch those well-meaning Christians in the face for quoting this verse at the wrong times. And sometimes I want to punch Paul in the face for having wrote it. Sorry, that's probably sacrilegious, but it's honest.

June 15, 2011 was one of those days.

A Phone Call

I was standing in line at Universal Mart. It is only a few miles from the airport. Shelli had just come to pick me up from the airport along with Chris Bosma, our super-intern, and Aubree Dell, our resident nurse. I had just returned from Ohio where I was with my mom's side of the family burying the patriarch of my family, Grandpa Roush as I knew him. He had lived 89 years. A few weeks prior, he had stopped eating. His time had come and his death was not unexpected, but it was still a great loss to the family. I was able to spend a lot of time with my mom, the oldest child in a family of five, and we had a sweet time together. I was looking forward to hugging my kids soon and talking late into the night with Shelli about all that I was thinking and feeling after the last three days in Ohio.

Suddenly the phone in my pocket rang. It was Pastor Pierre. That's nice, I thought, he is calling to make sure I got in and welcome me back.

"*Bonswa*," I answered.

"Aaron, it is Pastor. Jay has been in an accident."

I could tell from Pastor's voice that he was in a panic.

"I am driving him to Miami-Dade."

"Is it critical?"

I am not sure why I asked that question or where it came from. But it sounded serious, and I needed to know just how serious.

"No, I don't think so. I don't know. Kacie is with him; I have him in the Land Cruiser…we are driving there now. He says he can't feel his legs."

Holy crap. There may have been some other words that went through my head at the time.

"Okay, we are not far. We will meet you at the hospital."

Aubree, Chris and Shelli could tell from the look on my face that this was serious. We finished paying for our items, hopped back in the truck, and headed to the hospital. I updated them on the conversation, we all shared our fears and concerns, and then all that was left was to pray; Chris prayed out loud as I drove.

Carrying the Board

We arrived about seven minutes ahead of Pastor. We communicated to the ER personnel that another vehicle was coming with a serious injury, and I made sure the guards at the gate knew so that we didn't delay them at the door. When they arrived, it was a bit chaotic. I can remember the odd feeling I had at grabbing the board with Jay on it, oxygen attached, he clearly in pain. And I couldn't help but think that just two days prior I was carrying my grandfather's body in a casket almost in the same manner. It was eerie.

It is hard for me to capture the feelings over the next few hours. The minutes crept along very slowly. There are very poignant moments that stick out…giving Amy a hug as Jay was wheeled into x-ray, looking Kacie in the eye and seeing her in nurse mode while we waited, and the air of concern and shock among everyone as we allowed the care providers to do their work.

They took Jay into the ER, got IVs going, started pain meds, took him for x-rays, and started the process of getting Jay out of the country. It was clear right from the start that his injuries were serious and that the best course of action was to get him out of Haiti and to a place where they could offer better care. I was handed a phone and Jay's insurance information and that became my sole purpose on the earth—to do whatever I could to push the process with his insurance company to get the med-evacuation approved. I was thankful to have something to focus on and act on.

There were many challenges to getting Jay out of the country quickly. The insurance company had their processes of approval, which required their own doctors to evaluate the situation. That process takes time. Once it is approved, they have to get a hospital that is willing to take the patient, in this case, in Miami, Florida. I learned a lot over the next few hours, including that the cost of a flight like this would be around $11,000. Then there are the challenges of being in Haiti. A giant generator runs the airport, and they shut it down at 11:00 PM. That meant the flight would need to be here before then.

Jay is a remarkable man. My respect for him only increased as I had the privilege of living and working alongside him in Haiti. Always calm, seemingly unflappable, and always keeping Pastor and I on our toes with a joke right in the middle of a serious conversation. Jay was beloved and respected by the Haitians he worked alongside. He would always take the time to joke around and practice his Creole with the various work crews we had on campus, taking it upon himself to learn various, often obscure, Haitian proverbs. "*Sac vid pa konpe*" was often followed by "*chien gran gou pa jway*," which means "an empty sack won't stand" and "a hungry dog doesn't play."

Jay's presence and influence on campus cannot be underestimated.

Later we would learn that Jay had ten broken ribs, two pneumo-thoraxes in his lung, and two broken vertebrae. Although clearly in pain from his extensive injuries, he never lost his light spirit. In the midst of getting IVs, he motioned to Pastor to come near him so he could say something. Pastor leaned down to hear Jay whisper "*Ti Gro Moun.*" This was an on-going joke with Pastor and Jay. It means "little old man," not necessarily the best of compliments to a well-established Haitian man. Pastor just laughed. Later when it came time to load Jay into the plane, he looked straight at Chris and said "don't drop me, intern." Jay thought it was his duty to make sure the interns knew their place, even as he was being loaded into an air ambulance.

Arrangements

Rachel at Miami-Dade was amazing. She demonstrated a patient strength that I found to be a real gift. Usually someone in her position is overbearing and pushy, or too timid and not persistent enough. Rachel is the logistics coordinator for Miami-Dade and helped me to arrange the air ambulance. At some point she took over, for which I was most thankful. When we were facing the possibility of the airport closing, she made contact with someone at the UN who could exert influence and keep the airport open. Rachel communicated clearly and probably pushed the process as fast as it could go.

Unfortunately for all of us, Jay was not able to get the flight out that night. By the time it was approved and the arrangements were set in motion, it would be much too late. Jay would have to stay the night. The good news was that the flight would be in the air early from the States and on the ground in Haiti when the airport opened. We would leave the hospital at 7:00AM to take Jay to be flown out to Miami.

Germ-a-phobia Cure

When Chris came to us for the summer, he was a self-identified germ-a-phobe. Having lived in Haiti as long as I had, I chuckled and in my own not so gentle way saying, "Oh, we will cure you of that this summer." Jay and I had made it our personal goal actually to help Chris get over this mental block. We gave him little projects like cleaning out the back of a box truck where there were rats living or unloading a container that was filthy. We didn't expect rat droppings to actually fall in his mouth, but we just chalked it up to helping our intern grow as a person. Cleaning the chicken coop out was a huge feat for Chris up to this point. Little did I know that the actual moment in time that Chris would be cured would be this night, of all nights. After this night, Chris was no longer a germ-a-phobe.

It was decided that Chris and Nathan Pierre would stay the night at the hospital to be a support to Amy. Unfortunately for all of us on campus, we had nine college students arriving on Thursday—the next day. Forty-three more students were scheduled to arrive on Saturday, and another two would show up on Sunday. We were smack-dab in the middle of our busiest time of the summer. Chris and Nathan were young and deeply wanted to stay, so the decision was made. I took everyone else back to campus for a few hours of sleep before returning with a bag for Amy and making sure Jay got out okay.

Jay was eventually moved from one of the two beds in the ER to the ICU. There are four beds put closely together in the ICU, and Jay found himself between two patients. Chris was on duty with Jay in a chair between Jay and one of the other patients around 3:00 AM while Amy tried to get a little rest in a nearby dorm room. The patient next to Jay was clearly not well. He seemed to be suffering from some sort of stroke or head injury that caused him not to be in his right mind. He was stripped of all clothes except for a giant man-diaper. Occasionally the patient would get very agitated, writhe and scream, needing to be restrained. And more often than not, the patient would have his hand in the diaper, pulling it off, getting his bodily fluids all over his hands and spreading it around on himself. Anyone who has raised a toddler probably has some experience with this phenomenon. The ICU was not a place of rest for Jay this night.

The turning point for Chris occurred at some point this night. As he was looking after Jay, helping him stay as comfortable as possible, at one point catching his vomit as he was mobilized on his back and unable to move much beyond turning his neck, he sat quietly next to the disturbed man. Things were quiet and Chris was sitting unaware of the hand reaching out to him. Suddenly he felt the stroke of a finger along his check, and then the full palm of a hand rub his hair and slide down the full side of his other check.

The diaper man just wiped his entire hand all over his head.

"*M' pa T choo choo ou!*" Chris yelled as he grabbed the man's wrist and placed it back in his own bed space. Translated Chris said, "I am not your sweetheart!"

I was so proud of Chris as he relayed the story to me the next morning. Rather than totally freaking out, he calmly got up from his chair, walked across the room, doused his hands in sanitizer and calmly rubbed it all over his head and hands. I declared him no longer a germ-a-phobe from that point on.

Nathan made light of it the next day as well. Sitting across from Chris at lunch, he suddenly took a deep sniff and asked, "Does it smell like fresh diaper in here to anyone? Oh wait, that's your face!" In light of the heavy mood and lack of sleep over the last 24 hours, Chris and Nathan laughed until it hurt while the others around them, not knowing the story, just looked on in wonder.

Moving On

We watched from the tarmac as the Learjet took off for Miami with Jay and Amy on board. It was odd to watch them leave like they did. They left pretty much everything behind, including their kids. We on campus had no time to make sense of what just happened or grieve; we had teams arriving the next three days with all the expectations and hopes that short-term mission teams have. We now had the four Shultz children to look after.

Jay's accident truly was a freak occurrence. Jay was driving a John Deere Gator and joking around. His oldest son Jeremiah was in the passenger seat when they took a corner around the backhoe that Pastor Pierre was driving. Somehow Jay cut the corner too sharp or the Gator slipped on the loose rocks and Jay ended up twisted and pinned between the back arm of the backhoe and the seat of the gator. Jeremiah jumped clear when they hit. Jay instantly knew something was seriously wrong, struggling to breathe with his broken ribs and losing all feeling in his legs. He went so far as to say to Amy, "I'm sorry honey; I don't think I am going to make this one."

In the weeks that followed, the load was extremely heavy. Jay ended up having surgery in Miami where they fused his spine from T-6 to T-11. He made it to Indianapolis about a week later and started his rehab in the Rehab Hospital of Indianapolis. The two Shultz boys left a few weeks later with their Aunt Rita. Anna stayed behind with Fedlaine for another month. Fedlaine's adoption process was not yet complete, so she was without a passport and the ability to come back to the States. Things kept moving forward with the teams on campus.

It says in Isaiah 55:8 "'For your thoughts are not my thoughts, neither are your ways my ways,' declares the Lord." Clearly this was not the way any of us would choose for Jay, for Amy, for their family, for NVM, for anyone who was affected by this accident. It was strange though, especially when I heard myself say it the first time: If this accident was going to happen, it couldn't have happened to a better guy. What I mean by this is that Jay is the kind of person who will walk again. He has the kind of spirit, the kind of strength, and the kind of faith, to take an accident like this head on and make the most of life. Even if he were to never walk again, Jay will see his circumstance as an opportunity to glorify God.

I am proud to call him my friend.

And I suppose the load I ended up carrying as a result of the void Jay left wasn't more than I could handle. Looking back, I did what I had to do for all the people that came to NVM that summer and for the family and people around me. And God still did some amazing things with the teams that came.

When I consider the Shultz family today, I am still amazed at the grace in which they have handled this radical shift in their lives. In some ways, their lives are very different. But in all the ways that seem to really matter, they are still the same, fun-loving, Christ-centered, hospitable, caring family they always were. Why should Jay's accident change any of that?

Just consider yourself warned if you ever feel like quoting that verse to me in the midst of a great difficulty.

9 FEDLAINE

"God sets the lonely in families…"
-Psalm 68:2

At NVM, adoption of children from Haiti is not a goal or a focus of the orphan care portion of the ministry. Giving children the opportunity to grow up in Haiti, to be proud of who they are, to learn skills and develop their potentials in the context of loving homes is the focus. We educate the kids in our community, we provide health care, and for some, we provide a home. To date, there is only one child that has entered the process of being adopted by an American family. Her name is Fedlaine. Going forward, adoptions from Haiti through NVM will be the exception.

When I was asked to come to Haiti, I was asked to fill the role of mission team coordinator. I would take on responsibility for all the teams that came to Haiti, from the time that they landed at the airport until we dropped them back off for their return flight. I didn't know we would see over 900 people during the year. And I also didn't know that one of the questions I would ponder with God is whether or not we were here for just one child rather than the other 900 people.

Fedlaine

I still clearly remember meeting Fedlaine. I first came to Haiti in March of 2009. I was travelling with Aaron Sherrick, the guy running most things for NVM stateside at the time. He and I were down with two video guys who were donating their time and expertise to help tell the story of NVM. We were at the children's home getting video of Pastor and meeting the kids. This is when I met Fedlaine, or Fifi as I have come to know her.

Fifi was nearly three-and-a-half-years-old at the time. She was young, quiet, and there was something different about her. It may have been her skin, which was a much lighter shade than all the other kids in the home. She had the nickname of *"Ti Blan"* which means "little white kid," but I don't think that was what it was. I think it was something else, something intangible.

Fifi had lived a tough life up to the point she came into the home. She was basically neglected and abandoned by her parents. She would wander the village alone, scrounging for food where she could. She was aloof, avoided by the other kids, and was developing a reputation for being very mean. There were times in the day when she would crawl under a bush and lay down to sleep. One time Pastor found her and thought she may be dead only to find out she was sleeping very hard. The remnants of a fungal infection still lingered in the back of her head creating a big bald spot rather than allowing her beautiful black hair to grow. Malnutrition was having its impact, and she was rarely bathed or clean.

I apparently was not alone in feeling like there was something special about this little girl. Jay Shultz, the president of the board of NVM at the time, had been down and met Fifi. He came back to the States and told his wife Amy, "If we ever adopt a child, it will be this one." Something in Jay saw the great potential in Fifi, and his heart was quickly captured.

For whatever reason, Pastor asked the Shultzes if they would consider adopting Fedlaine. Again, it runs counter to the overall philosophy and ministry of NVM, but there it was. It didn't take but one meeting for Amy to spend time with Fedlaine and their hearts were fully enraptured. The Shultz family would go from five to six.

Moving Slowly

International adoption can be challenging. Shelli and I have been through the process with our son, Sitota, and we know the ups and downs you go through, especially emotionally. It is challenging enough when you have an adoption agency, but Jay and Amy decided to work with Pastor directly to get the necessary paperwork done. Amy came to visit with Fifi in the summer of 2010 and had a great visit, but you can imagine the difficulty in saying good-bye. For Fifi, she now had parents, but could not yet live with them. For Jay and Amy, once your heart is committed to a child as your own...the child IS your own. Just like a biological child, if you peel open a parent's heart, you will find no difference in their love and commitment to their child.

Certainly part of the motivation for moving to Haiti for the Shultz family was to take Fifi into their home and see the adoption to completion. I can remember one of them saying "We are not leaving without her." I thought Pastor may intentionally drag his feet to keep them in country longer because of all the great work they provide to NVM. And the adoption was moving very slowly. I think part of the reason was Pastor was so busy with trying to juggle all the responsibilities he carried with the ministry that he didn't always have time to push the smaller details forward. Another part was the reality that the Haitian government can sometimes move very slowly.

I don't want you to get the wrong impression though. The adoption of Fifi was by no means the only motivation. Jay always wanted to live overseas and do mission work, and he was perfectly suited for the role that NVM required. Jay had also become one of Pastor's best friends over the years, establishing that relationship before NVM started in 2005. As the Shultz family prayed and started to take steps of faith, God seemed to open the doors for them to come. It was a great day when they arrived here in country and took Fedlaine into their home as one of their own.

Transformation Continues

Fedlaine was already a different child from the one I met the first time in 2009. Having been loved and cared for in the NVM children's home, she had joy and hope in her life. She was attending the school on campus and beginning to learn her basics for kindergarten. She was much healthier physically, all infections were gone and there were no more signs of malnutrition. This transformation would only continue under the loving care of the Shultz family when she moved in with them in January.

Sitting down at dinner on one of our first nights, we had chicken. Fedlaine proceeded to pick clean her chicken bone, eating every morsel of substance she could. I'm talking clean like a dog would pick every last fiber of meat or substance until the bone was completely clean and dry. She then proceeded to do that with every other person's chicken in her family until she had six clean chicken bones piled up on her plate in front of her. Although she ate well in the children's home, she didn't get a lot of variety and clearly this girl liked her chicken. It was impressive.

What began to emerge as the year went on was a young girl full of energy and life. There were lots of changes initially, from living with her friends in the children's home, to now living with her family, bunking in with her older sister Anna in a tent. English was now the language she heard from the *blans* around her instead of the consistent Creole from her Haitian friends and caretakers. She continued to go to school at Nehemiah Christian Academy, and it seemed the consistent love and structure of a family, loving and caring for her, praying and singing to her when it was bedtime, was allowing the vibrant, energetic, rambunctious little girl to blossom.

Taking on Fifi

June 15, 2011 changed so much for so many, Fifi among them. On the morning of June 16th, Fedlaine's parents were on a LearJet on their way to Miami. Suddenly older sister Anna was taking on the parental role with Fedlaine, a tall order for a sixteen-year-old living in a foreign culture. The staff community immediately came around the kids, and Jay and Amy's extended family quickly organized to come down to Chambrun. Two weeks after Jay and Amy left, the two boys would return to the States with their aunt and uncle to live with their grandparents. Anna, when given the option to leave with her brothers or stay behind, chose to stay with Fedlaine.

Amy was able to return in mid-July, about four weeks after the accident. It was decided at that time that Anna would return with Amy back to the States, and Fifi would transition into our home. A bunk bed replaced Sitota's twin bed in his room, and Fifi moved all her stuff to our house. She was initially very excited to be moving in with us, lessening the obvious concern and sadness that Amy was feeling. I still can't imagine what Amy was going through, a husband recovering from back surgery and now paralyzed from the waist down, a sixteen-year-old daughter who has played the role of mother for a month who was not ready to leave Haiti or her sister, and now leaving behind their youngest daughter after five months of having her. Heart-wrenching just doesn't quite describe it.

Graces along the way

Grace is defined as "unmerited favor." Caring for Fifi has not been without its graces. On September 18th, Fifi happened to lose her first tooth. The tooth was at the point where a strong breeze could probably blow it out, so I was the lucky one who got to pull it out before dinner one night. Amy was here on a visit with Fedlaine and got to be present for this big moment in her child's life. She could have lost the tooth anytime, but it happened while her mom was here. Once she started losing teeth, she apparently couldn't stop; Fedlaine lost two more teeth over the next three days. I kept singing that all she wanted for Christmas was her two front teeth!

Another grace has been the presence of the Warner family. Jim and Cheryl Warner moved to campus with Janessa and Jaime, their two daughters, at the end of May. They are staff with Global Aid Network (www.gainusa.org) under Cru (www.ccci.org). Jim and Cheryl have adopted five girls all together, all from other countries. They know all the challenges of raising girls, especially girls coming from challenging backgrounds in their countries of birth. Their youngest daughter, Janessa, has become quite a friend and caretaker to all the kids on campus. Jim and Cheryl had tremendous challenges adopting Janessa from Jamaica that demanded much perseverance and patience. We could not have hand-picked a better couple to be a source of support and experience for what we would go through with Fifi.

Technology has been another huge grace. With communication tools like Skype and e-mail, we were able to allow Fifi to stay connected to her family at home in ways that were not possible even ten years ago. Fifi still struggled at times to talk over the video to her family, but the evenings when they were able to see one another, hear each other's voices, and tell one another they loved each other were extremely important and helpful.

Jay's Return

One other tremendous grace was the return of Jay and Amy to campus on November 9, 2011. It is tough to measure and describe the impact of Jay's presence on campus. The day before they arrived, Lupson, one of our maintenance guys, saw that we were getting a hand crank cart out to see if it would work for Jay. On the surface, Lupson looks like a hard, strong, stoic Haitian. If I didn't know Lupson like I do, I would be afraid to meet him in a dark alley. When we explained, again, that Jay can't walk and the cart was for jay, tears began to fill his eyes as he walked away.

When Jay arrived, it was amazing to watch him care for our community of folks. His upbeat spirit is infectious. I became his chauffer on the very Gator in which he had his accident and drove him out to the construction site. He quickly had a group of construction guys laughing it up with him as they reconnected. As we made our way across campus, the school kids headed to recess surrounded him as he made high fives and said hello.

I took time to notice those on campus viewing Jay from a distance, this look of sadness and almost pity when they were not with him. You couldn't find any of that look in Jay's eyes. He was just happy to see everyone.

Jay's presence, along with Amy's, was calming and stabilizing for Fifi as she went through yet another transition. They were here to celebrate her birthday and help her go from our house to living with the Warners. They would return to the States two days after we left, still waiting for paperwork to be signed.

Hope to Come

At the time of writing, Fifi is still in Haiti. She is now in the care of the Warner family, spending much of her time with Janessa Warner. We continue to pray for the adoption paperwork to be complete and for her safe journey to live with her family in Indiana. That day simply cannot come fast enough. Frankly, of all the things we have faced this year, the challenges of getting Fifi home have weighed most heavily on my heart. This has been the toughest chapter to write as I consider all this little girl has been through, and how much their family longs to be together.

The one thing that keeps me going is to imagine waiting for her to come walking down the hallway at the airport, family and friends waiting to give her huge hugs and welcome her home. We will be there waiting, with tears in our eyes, as she finally makes it home. And I picture our families together, cooking out, enjoying the Indiana summer, our girls playing together like they did in Haiti. Or perhaps one day as teenagers, talking about boys, or picking on their brothers together.

It says in Romans 5:3-5 that "we also rejoice in our sufferings, because we know that suffering produces perseverance; perseverance, character; and character, hope. And hope does not disappoint us, because God has poured out his love into our hearts by the Holy Spirit, whom he has given us." We will not stop persevering until Fedlaine is home, and the hope we have for that day will not disappoint. It will be a great day indeed.

10 A GREAT MORNING IN HAITI

Aug 20, 2011

The day started like many days had over the past year. The generator kicked off early in the morning. I pulled myself out of bed as the temperature began to rise with the sun coming up. It was still before six o'clock. I found Pastor outside, and he had decided to shut off the generator to conserve fuel. I told him that, while I agreed with his reasoning for turning it off, a little communication with everyone on campus would have been helpful prior to shutting it down. He quickly recognized that no morning showers, no working toilets, no running water, and not sleeping in on a Saturday for a staff that had been expecting a little extra sleep could prove problematic for him. For once, I was just glad the generator wasn't off because of a clogged fuel filter. Pastor Pierre turned the generator back on.

I went back to bed for a little while, but as my kids started to get up, I got up and tried to shuffle them out of Mom's room. Sleeping in was a long forgotten reality. When your home is only 600 square feet, it can be tough to get any alone time, let alone quiet. I was able to get the kids out fairly quietly and was excited to find Jim at work making waffles in the kitchen. My kids love waffles, almost as much as I do, and so this was a Saturday morning treat. Thankfully, Shelli was able to stay in bed.

Frisbee Challenge

As the morning wore on and the waffles were devoured, we started to look for things to do. Someone had discovered an Aerobie, one of those little frisbee like things that, if thrown properly, can go for nearly a mile. Sitota discovered that he could chuck it pretty far, so he was enjoying himself, tossing it up and chasing after it. I decided that I would test the world record for distance with the thing. It was a little windy, and it was in my face, so I aimed for the hospital from the sidewalk near the women's dorm and let her fly. The Aerobie took off and, frankly, far exceeded my expectations. The wind helped it sail over a tree, and then just as it was heading down, another gust sent it up almost over the newly-installed roof of the hospital. One of the nurses who was on the playground with some Haitians said I nearly cleared the roof altogether. Of course, this left me with a new challenge: climbing up on the roof to get it down.

All of this was part of my master plan to waste time and hang out with my kids. Two of my kids were following me around making sure I didn't fall off, hoping to get their hands on the Aerobie next. As I wound my way up through the trusses and onto the roof, I realized I had quite a view from up there. I was almost as high as the warehouse. I shuffled over to the Aerobie, only to let it fly back in the direction of the dorms. This time the wind did not play in my favor, and the Aerobie quickly found its way to the top of the tree. Another challenge.

Slowly I worked my way back down from the roof and back into the field next to the hospital. As I made my way over to the tree, a small crowd began to gather. I couldn't help but think that this could be very entertaining for some of the Haitians that were watching…how is Aaron going to get this thing out of the tree now? I tried shaking it, to no avail. I then noticed that there was a branch that was barely hanging on, and probably long enough to reach where the Aerobie was stuck, so I started to work the branch back and forth to break it. At this point, Ericson decided that I needed a machete and ran off to get one from his dad. Now Ericson is a great kid, about eight-years-old, but he isn't the brightest kid. I don't know how he got his nickname, but it is Bozo, and it seems to fit him. The image of Bozo running across the campus all crazy like only an eight-year-old boy can, with a machete swinging by his side, will stick in my head for a long, long time.

As Bozo got back, he quickly took the first few hacks at the branch. He made a little progress, but not much. He next handed it over to me, and I took a few swings. "Not bad" I thought as I nearly chopped it through. I stopped to let someone else take a turn when Mika stepped up. Mika is one of our housekeeping staff. She is very meek, rather shy and soft-spoken. But as soon as she had the machete in her hand, it was like a finely-tuned weapon in the hand of a skilled expert. Her wrist would snap at just the right moment as she quickly finished off the branch. "Whoa…don't mess with Mika with a machete in her hand," was all I was thinking now. In no time, we had the Aerobie out of the tree, and Sitota was entertaining himself again, flinging it in the air, but nowhere near a tree.

Hurting to Healing

I found my way over to the playground to hang out a little while. That is where I got the story on the little Haitian girl that was playing with the nurses. Her name is Elderley (Ed ul lee). Apparently Elderley came to our clinic over a month ago straight from nearly a month stay at the General Hospital in downtown Port-au-Prince. She has some sort of skin disease that they were trying to treat without success. Finally, after exhausting what they thought they were able to do, they released little Elderley saying there was nothing they could do for her. But they did tell her to find a Dr. Edmond in a little clinic in Chambrun and that she may be able to help her. I have no idea how someone at the general hospital in downtown had heard of our doctor or our clinic or why they thought we could help, but I was stunned.

Elderley is a little girl with sores all over her body. The sores were often open and extremely painful. Aubree said that it looked almost like she had been burned when she first arrived. It was really unclear what they were to do with her, but one of our medical interns (a young man who had just finished his first year of med school) went to work researching and trying to find what might be causing the sores. As time went by, our medical folks settled on an auto-immune diagnosis. I didn't fully understand the medical parts of it, but they decided to find a pretty rare drug that is designed to help treat leprosy. They found it in the States, had a team bring it down, and started treating little Elderly with it. The deal Aubree made with her is that we would treat her, and someday when the sores were better, she would come back and they would play on the new playground together.

Apparently today was that day.

Elderley was wearing her very best dress, and her father had brought her all the way from Delmas to play on the playground. The medicine they were giving her was helping her get better, enough that she was able to run, jump, climb, slide, and do all the other normal things a young girl would do on a playground. It was still evident that her body was dealing with something, but it didn't prevent her from playing like a normal child anymore. The nurses were beaming with pride at their little friend who was getting better. Our medical folks see a lot of sick people and deal with death on a weekly basis. So to see a young patient who makes such remarkable strides, especially after being told by others that there was nothing they could do, that feels good. That is a treasure we celebrate and hold on to, especially in the discouraging times.

Just Add Water

We ended up having a water balloon fight. I think everyone had the

69

most fun pelting me. I am not sure why I deserved everyone ganging up on me, but it was a fun activity on an otherwise hot day. Someone had a water gun, and it of course ended up in Sitota's hands. He took great pride in shooting as many people as he could. Something about that child makes it possible for everyone to gladly take his little sprays of water and enjoy it. And none of the other kids around here were trying to get the gun.

Probably the best part of the morning, at least as far as Shelli was concerned, was that she didn't get up until late into the morning. A first for our time in Haiti, and much deserved.

God is so good, all the time. And I suppose this day I was reminded by how normal the day felt. The sun was shining, friends were around, we were celebrating the discovery of the right medicine to help a young child get better from a nasty illness, we laughed and played and otherwise had a normal day. I suppose it felt so atypical and stands out because of how often the days are less than normal. Regardless of the reasons, it was a great morning. And I was grateful.

11 LIGHTNING STRIKES

I wish I were making this stuff up. I really do. How many seemingly crazy things can happen in one year?

September 19, 2011

It had been a good day. It was Monday, and I had just finished up showing the Haitian staff how to score goals on the soccer field. I may be 35, but there are still flashes of the former all-conference college soccer player in me. We won seven to four, and I scored three of our goals. I suppose it wasn't an exercise in personal humility. I was playfully teasing some of my friends on the other team. Regardless, we had fun playing, and many others were sitting around watching. We finished up the game in time for most of the staff to shower up before dinner.

Dinner starts around 6:00, and by 6:15, we were sitting down enjoying an all too rare beef roast. Many of the Haitian staff had not wandered in yet. A strong thunderstorm had rolled in, and it was raining pretty hard. Maybe that was what was keeping them. Haitians typically do not like being out in the rain. I mean, who does really, especially when it is a storm?

Lightning Strikes

Suddenly there was a flash of lightning followed by an immediate crack of thunder. Everyone at the table in the dining hall was immediately shaken. It was so loud and powerful and completely unexpected. After calming the kids a bit and taking stock of everyone, I stuck my head outside to look at the girl's bathhouse, thinking the lighting must have hit something nearby. No hole in the roof. I noticed the cross on the school across the way was still there. It must not have hit there either. I knew it

71

wasn't the generator because we still had power. I went back inside and sat down to eat.

About five minutes went by when one of our Haitian staff came in and said that Gestin was calling for help. Gestin is our community liaison. I was having trouble getting clear information, but something in my Spirit sensed that things were not right, so I sent Aubree and our medical staff out. Kacie, a nurse who lived and worked at Nehemiah for a year, half the time we were there, happened to be in town for a visit and was the first one out the door. I confirmed with her later that she sensed something was not right either and took off out the door.

I followed the medical folks outside, collecting a flashlight as I went. As I rounded the corner of the container that serves as the office/storage for the Jesus Film Project, I came to find them already hard at work half-way to our gate that leads to Chambrun. They were working on someone who was lying on the ground. As I approached, I discovered that they were doing CPR, thirty compressions to two breaths.

Holy crap. I have never actually seen CPR done on a person before.

It turns out that the giant lightning strike hit Jocelyn, one of our security guards. He had just completed his shift, had turned things over to the next guy on duty, and was on his way home walking off campus when he was struck.

Our medical staff went into fast action, starting CPR, getting him on a board, bringing the oxygen. As I think back, it was actually impressive to watch them work. Adam was without a shirt, having removed it to serve as a support for Jocelyn's head. A couple of the nurses had run for the crash kit and board they put together, having learned to be prepared for an emergency from prior experience. Flip flops had been lost in the mud and rain as they ran for supplies or help. Others were holding flashlights, clearing space. We sent Michel to get the truck so that we could be ready to move him and get him on the way to the hospital. I told everyone who wasn't medical to please stand back and to pray. Rain continued to pour down on everything.

He was quickly placed on the board. I helped put the board in place and fastened one of the straps around his thighs. He was loaded up in the back of a truck. Once we got everyone in, there were seven people in the back of the truck, plus Jocelyn. Michel was driving, and the last thing I told him just before he took off was "Drive SAFE, but FAST."

There was a split second, just as they had put Jocelyn in the back of the truck and as they were giving instructions to Michel when I thought about pulling him out of the driver's seat and jumping in there myself. This would have made trip number five for me, racing to the hospital. But in that fraction of a second, I thought about how it was dark, raining, and that they may be taking him to a closer hospital that I didn't know. Michel is a good driver (as long as he is not going in reverse), and I chose in that fraction of a second to let him go. And there was a part of me that breathed a sigh of relief. For me, the emergency was over.

I went back and checked in with Shelli. What is the most useful thing I could do right now? There were at least twelve people in that one truck. It is raining. They are going to need a ride home, and they will not want to ride in the back of the truck in the rain. I can follow behind them. The Land Cruiser has the most interior space, so I decided to take it. Shelli immediately thought about a change of clothes. I grabbed a shirt for Adam, and Shelli grabbed five changes of clothes for the nurses. I didn't want to go by myself, so I grabbed one of our Haitian staff to ride with me.

A Not Very Nice Dream Fulfilled

I made a big mistake when I headed out. I headed through town. Thankfully the team went the back way around to the hospital. I was making extremely slow time, even with my aggressive driving. It was frustrating.

I am not sure what this says about me, but I have always wanted to be driving a vehicle and guide it through a giant puddle only to spray some innocent bystanders on the road. Okay, not innocent, preferably someone I really didn't like. Anytime I find giant puddles in a vehicle, which is often in Haiti, I will try and hit them and watch the spray fly, but only if I know the road. Sometimes the puddle could actually be hiding a very dangerous and deep pothole. And If I see people, I slow down or avoid them. I just can't bring myself to actually spray someone.

Due to very poor infrastructure in Haiti where roads do not have sewers to guide the rain, and to the massive deforestation of the mountains, the rain water simply runs across the top of the ground and through the streets causing great flooding in Port-au-Prince. This night, it had been raining long and hard and the streets were covered. As we drove along and encountered another long line of cars, I veered left of the line and proceeded to pass the cars along the left side. As I did, I passed a motorcycle with three people on it. Did I just spray them? By the look on Feance's face, it was clear I did. Then I noticed the line of people walking on the sidewalk to the left of me, and then I noticed the rooster tail spray coming from our truck. With nowhere to hide, I am pretty sure the spray went higher than their heads. I slowed down a little to try and reduce the spray, but no way was I stopping at this point. These people may be really mad at me. I just totally drenched them.

I felt bad. I really did. But this was an emergency, or so I told myself. And I really didn't mean for it to happen, it just did. I'm not sure why I put this in here, only to point out that funny little things happen even in the midst of a crisis.

Odd Little Things

The ride to the hospital was a wild one for those in the back of the truck, as you can imagine. They were holding on to one another, switching places at times to trade who was doing chest compressions and who was doing the breathing. There was one time they were afraid they had lost E'Tienne out the side of the truck. It was wet, cold, dark, and difficult work. But they made it there in good time, probably less than 45 minutes. The medical staff continued to work on him for another ten to fifteen minutes when they arrived at the hospital.

Jocelyn never revived.

When Pastor called later, having now been sitting in traffic for twenty minutes without moving, I shared that I was in Fleuriot. He said that Gestin, our community liaison, was with the family on campus, and they needed to come to the hospital to sign some paperwork and retrieve Jocelyn's body. I pulled a u-turn and headed back.

There are many little things from that night that stand out...odd little things. For example, the vehicle I was driving was completely out of gas. The gas light had been on since I left the campus. I am not sure how I did not run out, and when I got back to campus, we couldn't find the key to the gas pump. I thought I had it at one point and walked around to the pump to try and unlock it. When I was unsuccessful, we determined we needed to go to Chambrun to get the key from one of our staff. This process of getting to Chambrun, retrieving the key and returning, took ten minutes. That entire ten minutes, my cheap little Haitian cell phone sat submersed in a puddle next to the gas pump. I apparently thought I dropped it in my pocket, only to actually drop it in the mud. I pulled it out, and what do you know, it still was on and working. It still works to this day. I thought about trying the same test on my iPhone, but I lack the courage.

The other odd thing was that most of our team in the back of the truck saw a rainbow. They had just turned left towards Port-au-Prince when one of them saw it, pointed it out, and the rest saw it too. I say this is odd because the sun set at 5:48 PM that night, probably a full hour before the time they saw it. Not to mention it was raining. There is such a thing as a "moonbow," where the sunlight reflecting off the moon is strong enough to cast a rainbow. Is this what they saw? I do know I was praying that God would send angels (Hebrews 1:14) to watch over the vehicle, to keep them safe and to guide them as they went. I like to believe this was a sign of God's hope to my friends in the back of the truck.

I took the long way around to the hospital, which was actually the short way this night, once I got the family loaded and the truck fueled. I was with the family and my friends when they saw Jocelyn's body. He looked peaceful. And we are confident he died instantly in spite of our teams heroic efforts. He had many burn marks, his pants were burnt, especially at the zipper, and his cell phone in his pocket was completely fried. He even smelled burnt.

Pastor took the family and his body to the morgue in Croix-des-Bouquets. We were back on campus and cleaned up by 11:30 P.M. that night.

The Next Day

We had a memorial service on campus the next day. Pastor gathered our staff and invited those in the community to be together in the church. It was sad and a bit surreal, but good to be together. I think everyone was still basically in shock. Pastor told all the workers that there would not be any work today and sent the crews home. Immediately after the service, I left for the airport. Three people from our partners in Germany were arriving, and I went to pick them up.

I sent an e-mail to my prayer team. I have over 80 people that I try and faithfully share my heart with and ask for prayer on a weekly basis. I called on this team many times over the year in instances like this. They are always a source of strength and encouragement to me. As I sent the e-mail letting them know what happened, I received many beautiful replies. One sticks out with poignancy and helped me realize the reality I am living:

We seem to live in a world (here in IN) where the fragility of life is somewhat "masked." We have the resources (food, money, education, medical care) to avert some problems, and we dial 9-1-1 when life gets out of control to let the "professionals" handle our emergencies (and, as you know, these props we have in place often hinder our ability to rely on God for all things). You all have had a front-row seat to the fragility of life since you arrived in Haiti last November.

My prayer is that God will give you what you need to get through today, and that He will never let you forget the ways that you have experienced His hand holding all things together…..even when they appear to be falling apart.

God be with you all today….

I will be honest. At this point in my year, I was longing for the "masking" of life. I was tired and ready for a few "professionals." And yet, there was part of me that was still thankful for the opportunity to live by faith. Back home, I think too many people live lives where there is no opportunity to really trust in God. You can trust in jobs, bank accounts, professional services, education…so many things. When you are in the middle of rural Haiti and lightning strikes, there isn't much to fall back on other than your faith in God. And until I was left with nothing but my faith, I am not sure I appreciated the real value of it. I suppose it is a piece of what Jesus talks about in discovering His Kingdom:

The Kingdom of Heaven is like treasure hidden in a field. When a man found it, he hid it again, and then in his joy went and sold all he had and bought that field. Again, the kingdom of heaven is like a merchant looking for fine pearls. When he found one of great value, he went away and sold everything he had and bought it.
    -Matthew 13:44-46

*For a personal account of these events from one of our medical staff, see appendix 1. It includes her experience at the funeral that took place on Saturday, September 24, 2011.

12 PENDULUM

Stretch Your Heart

There is a concept I was introduced to many years ago by one of the men I consider a mentor. It is the idea of how your heart grows. Like a rubber band that you stretch in one direction, it doesn't quite return to its original shape. It grows. Have you ever seen a big, thick rubber band that has been too long wrapped around something large? It becomes all goofy and stretched. Or maybe a deflated balloon…all stretched out and ragged? The concept goes that, as we stretch our hearts and feel the pain and hurting in the world, we also begin to have a larger capacity for love and mercy in the world. As you stretch in one direction, you also make room and capacity in the other. The more pain you face, when dealt with well, the more capacity for love and mercy. And the more love and joy you experience, the more willing and able you are to enter into pain. Of course, this was said in the context of being a follower of Christ and allowing God to help mold and stretch us. I have seen lots of people who have experienced pain and suffering, and it has left them bitter and angry. Allowing God's Spirit to work in us is an integral component.

NVM is an organization that is focused on development. We want to help Haitians move from darkness to light, from hopelessness to eternal life. We seek to focus on the work that God is doing in a person's life and help them become everything God would have them be. Moments of great joy and moments of great suffering are all filled with the potential for each of us to become who God would have us be. But never did I think I would experience such a pendulum of experiences and emotions as I have this year in such a short period of time. One day I experience something of great joy, and then the next day something extremely difficult. Or sometimes I experience both in the same event. Or even sometimes, I experience the highs and lows separately, but mere minutes apart. Maybe some stories will illustrate what I mean.

Life & Death

On June 7th, Shelli and I celebrated thirteen years of marriage together. We had planned to quietly let this marker in our lives together pass on by, but a few on campus decided to make dinner a special event. A separate table was set up, Nathan Pierre and Chris Bosma became our personal servers, others looked after our kids, and we actually sat through the entire meal. For those with young kids, the idea of sitting through an entire meal is like a gift from heaven. Usually dinner is comprised of picking up dropped utensils, refilling empty drinks, cleaning up a spill, or any number of possibilities that prohibit actually sitting through a meal. There was singing (some college students sang a special song), there was a toast (compliments of Jay Shultz), there was even a special dessert (giant chocolate chip cookie). The kids had made us special cards. The Haitians were introduced to the American wedding tradition of tapping on glasses to get the bride and groom to kiss…there was lots of tapping. It was an incredibly fun, memorable evening. Shelli and I felt very honored and loved and really enjoyed the life we share together.

The next day I got a phone call that my grandfather had passed away. He was eighty-nine years old, in failing health, and it was not entirely unexpected, but it was still a blow. This particular grandfather was the patriarch on my mom's side of the family. With five kids, he very much was the rock and center piece of the family. He was also a major influence on my life, especially as a kid growing up. I immediately made plans to get to Ohio to be with the extended family during the funeral. I left that Sunday arriving in time for the Monday funeral.

As you know from a previous chapter, I arrived back on a Wednesday, the 15th of June, the day Jay had his accident. And the weekend that followed, we welcomed close to 50 new people to campus, people who had NOT experienced the tragedy that was still very fresh for all of us, people with lots of excitement and energy, most of them visiting Haiti for the first time.

From life to death in two days …the pendulum swings.

A Stolen Beach Day

On July 4th, we were at the beach. It was one of those beautiful, pristine, Haitian summer days. The water was as clear as I have seen it, and I was reminded of the beauty of this Caribbean island. Days like this make me believe that Haiti can once again be the Pearl of the Caribbean. We relaxed and had a great time.

The next day, July 5th, I participated in a series of meetings with Pastor Pierre and our staff. Apparently one of our staff was stealing hygiene kits and water bottles from the warehouse, taking them to Port-au-Prince, and selling them. Another staff member was driving him and the stuff off campus and claiming that he didn't know the first staff member was stealing them. Pastor had sniffed out what was happening and was dealing with the very complicated situation. I say complicated because there are many things at work here.

On the one hand, Pastor understands those who are in poverty and their mentality. He understands why a person would be tempted to steal. So there was a level of compassion that Pastor was feeling. On the other hand, there was trust that was broken. Pastor is always quick to meet a need, especially among his staff, if only they ask. Our community in Chambrun and our staff are always our first priority in meeting needs.

Then there is the practical issue of firing them. If you fire them, they know NVM and may decide to come back and make things worse by stealing more or who knows what. Shortly after our arrival, I visited a partner ministry that had their computers stolen the night before. "Coincidentally" they had let a staff member go the night before. Plus we had invested a lot in these staff members, all of which would be lost.

But if we do nothing, then there is concern that we are setting a precedent that a person can get away with anything around here. Even if you are caught, there will not be any consequences. What is the right route to go? What makes sense biblically and culturally?

Pastor decided to go the route of forgiveness, and I was super impressed with the process he went through to get there. He confronted the two staff directly over many hours, talking through what they had done and what his options were. He had his friend who is the police chief of the station just up the road stop by. He had the chief explain the law and that according to the law, he could have both of them arrested and press charges. Pastor let his chief friend know that he would handle it internally, but would call him if he needed anything. He next called all the staff into his office and shared exactly what happened, that the two staff were stealing and that they were being restored. There was a short discussion among the staff, mostly regarding security on campus, and they closed with prayer. I can still remember the heaviness of the room as everyone shuffled out of Pastor's office.

I almost forgot all the fun and relaxing I had just had the day before as I tried to make sense of what just happened. As light and fun as the previous day was, this day was heavy. I was surprised how personally I took the fact that these guys were stealing. It was like they stole directly from me. How could they do that, especially when Shelli and I had given up so much to come and serve here! And I felt so challenged to forgive too. Pastor did not have to keep them on staff. He could have had them arrested. And he did not have to forgive them like he did. Yet Pastor chose the route of forgiveness and restoration, and looking back, it seems like the wise choice. It was probably the one that took the most courage.

I also had to work through my friendships and relationships with each of the staff. Was this place safe? Especially if people I work with are stealing? I believe in forgiveness, but his was hard, especially when I felt like no one would have argued with a decision to prosecute or fire our staff. How will I relate to them the next time I see them over lunch?

The pendulum in my own heart continued to swing for some time on this one. But what has been really surprising is how far it can swing in just a few moments.

A Matter of Minutes

It was the week after Easter, Sunday to be exact. I had popped into the office quickly to check my e-mail before I headed to the airport. In the moments I had to check my e-mail, I found some news that moved me almost to tears. These were not tears of sadness, but of joy and astonishment. A woman who was down here in January had heard and seen what we were doing with the two children's homes and knew that there were plans for two more. She committed to raising money to build the additional two and had just e-mailed to let us know that she had already raised the $150,000 needed to build the other two homes. That means that 64 more vulnerable, neglected, hungry kids could have a safe place to grow up. I immediately began to share the incredible news with other staff.

As I was outside, I saw Aubree and shared the news with her. We got separated in some different conversations, but then a few moments later we were talking again. This time Aubree was relaying to me that she just spoke to the police officer who was there and learned that the man we tried to save on Easter had died. What?! Indeed, this was the moment that I learned the man we worked so hard to save on Easter had actually died. Minutes apart from the good news I was sharing.

I gave Aubree a hug as we both felt the weight of this news, and next thing I know I am driving down the road to take our latest intern back to the airport. Her three months were up. One of the challenges of this work in Haiti is that you get to know and experience some pretty amazing things, life-changing things with people who come to visit. Interns especially who stay for longer periods of time, in this case three months, take up a special place in our hearts. I immediately went from joy, to sadness, to saying good-bye and asking what this intern will be looking forward to next.

A Long Obedience

If you had told me at the beginning of the year all the ways I would feel my heart being tugged, I am not sure I would have believed you. The pendulum can swing from one extreme to the next in mere minutes. There are more stories than could be told here. There was flooding one night where Pastor was almost washed away in his Land Cruiser, only to make it out with a three-week-old baby and her mother safely rescued while many other people died that night. There are countless stories from our medical clinic of a child who is improving, followed by the next horrible story of another preventable and curable disease in the next patient. Or stories from time spent in the village where hope and despair are found cohabitating. It is all around me.

I remember my Pastor from Indiana quoting author Brennan Manning in a sermon once. Brennan described the Christian life as "a long obedience in the same direction." When I take a long view of what I experience in the moments, and when I take each moment one at a time, I think I have found a way to not only persevere, but also to be fully present to what is in front of me. But it requires me to be fully present at every moment. Paul challenged us to "Rejoice with those who rejoice; mourn with those who mourn" (Romans 12:15). What a challenge this has become! I only pray I am thankful for it all, the good and the challenging stuff, and that I am fully present in each moment, even as the pendulum swings.

13 VOODOO IS IN THE AIR

There is a cultural reality that influenced our year in significant ways that deserves some conversation. Starting in the first chapter of this book, surrounding the narrative of Pastor's birth into the world, you hear the influence of witchdoctors and voodoo. Throughout our year, we continually encountered beliefs and behaviors that grow out of a culture heavily influenced by voodoo.

It is not my intention to describe the history and practice of voodoo. There are plenty of sources you can access through a simple internet search that will give you an overview of the history and dogma. You will discover that voodoo is a mixture of religion carried over from Western Africa with influences from Catholicism, combined with medicinal practice by rural "doctors" whose influence and power has been culturally reinforced for nearly 200 years. Voodoo and its influence is very real.

Sometimes teams that come down would ask about voodoo. "Is it real?" This is a silly question if you are a Haitian. It would be like asking an American "is freedom real?" We would struggle to really understand the question because freedom is such a part of the fabric of our lives that we would have a hard time comprehending it NOT being a reality, even if an alternative is offered as an example.

I have had many Christian African friends come to my home and church over the years. A question I often ask is what they see as holding Americans back from truly living as Christians in the world. Without fail, at the top of nearly every list of answers I have heard is a comment on the materialism in our culture. America has this large influence operating in the culture, at least in the suburban culture where I live, that says "buy! You must have more!" It is so prevalent, you may even say it is in the air we breathe, and those of us who live in it hardly notice it. But those who come in from the outside "smell" it immediately.

Voodoo is like that in Haiti. It is in the air you breathe. And it had influence all throughout our year. The difference is that most of the teams coming from America don't "smell" it.

Renouncing Voodoo

The second time I was in Haiti was in February 2010. I was leading a medical team from our church in providing mobile clinics to the thousands upon thousands of people living in the makeshift camps following the earthquake. It was only five weeks after the earthquake, and there was still great need. We returned home after our week of service, having seen nearly 2000 patients, and immediately handed over the knowledge and experience we had to our next team leaving a few days later.

Our next team had a very unique encounter right from the beginning. They arrived on a Saturday and got settled in at Pastor's house. On Sunday they drove out to church in Chambrun. Unbeknownst to them, a witchdoctor in the community had a dream the night before that told her to "go see the white missionaries." The witchdoctor showed up early the morning and sought Pastor Pierre out. Pastor led her to a relationship with Christ and to renounce witchcraft and voodoo. Pastor then made the decision to allow this witchdoctor to share her story in front of the church. The attention and authority the community gave to this woman was palpable. She shared her story of giving her life to Christ and renouncing her former ways.

After church, Pastor led the community to the village where they brought out the fetishes and implements of voodoo that the witchdoctor had in her home, and they burned them. A worship service broke out among the community there. Needless to say, our little team of medical folks was far from home. A dream sent a witchdoctor to church, and now they were destroying fetishes in the context of a mud hut village while pastor led the community in worship songs. As Dorothy from the Wizard of Oz might say, "we're not in Kansas anymore."

We have another former witchdoctor on our staff. His name is Legros Merius, and he was our security guard at one of our gates. He used to be one of the most powerful and sought out witchdoctors in the area. People would come from as far away as Cap-Haitian, sometimes a seven hour trip by vehicle on bumpy, Haitian roads, to seek out his influence and help. When Pastor started the church here, his wife started to attend. Soon after, the family started to come and ended up giving their lives to Christ. Pastor tells of burning all his fetishes and their renouncing voodoo and witchcraft. Two of his adult children also work for NVM now.

Chambrun

Pastor says there are still seventeen voodoo temples in Chambrun. They take on various forms and sizes, but voodoo is still a strong influence in the community where we lived. I saw Pastor Pierre interact with one of the witchdoctors at one of the larger temples one time. They are friends and get along well. I credit Pastor's wisdom and relational ability to preach and stand for something very different, but do it in a loving way. He asked the witchdoctor if he was ready to give his life to Christ, and he answered "not yet."

Aubree Dell was in the village one time and asked Eliana, one of our staff, what happens in the voodoo temple where this man was the witchdoctor. She said in dismissive sort of way, indicating her desire NOT to pursue this conversation further, "They feed the devil in there. Don't ever go in there."

Another time, Aubree was in the village and witnessed a "healing" ceremony. A woman who was sick arrived on a moto, and the "healing" process began. Four men met her outside and began by spitting in her face. Next they beat her. Then they poured water on her and slapped her. Then they lit a torch and circled her body with it, touching both sides of her head and under her feet. Then the head person pulled out a whip and started beating her with the whip. After the whipping, they poured some more water and some unknown liquid over her head, showered her with dirt, and then took her inside the temple to continue to process. You can imagine the feelings Aubree was having as a medical care provider watching this "healing" taking place[1].

There are many beliefs about the causes of illness in Haiti that are spiritual in nature, not physical. We encounter them often in our clinic and are grateful for the decision and philosophy of NVM that will ensure our hospital is a Haitian hospital. Without the knowledge of the culture, we would often treat in inappropriate ways. For example, many believe that their illness is caused by voodoo. Maybe someone has put a curse on you or maybe you have developed what is known as *move san*, or bad blood, as a result of a fight they were in three weeks ago. If your illness is caused by voodoo, and your skin is penetrated by a needle (as in administering medicine with a shot), then you will die. Fortunately, our Haitian doctor has the understanding and authority to treat our patients and help them in appropriate ways.

Spikes in Density

[1] For an account of what happened in Aubree's own words, see her blog at www.aubreedell.wordpress.com, entry for February 17, 2011. I have included a portion of her blog in Appendix 2.

There are a few times of the year when voodoo practice seems to spike in its intensity. At least from my short year, I observed it more readily a number of times. On Good Friday for example, there is a traditional dance, almost like a parade, that is called a Rara. People participating bring all number of instruments, and they march from village to village playing. People in the community will pay them to come and play in front of their house or in their area. The leader dances in front and cracks a whip, violently at times. One Rara shuffled by our campus in the direction of Chambrun, and I kept thinking the leader was going to accidently hit someone with his whip. Voodoo ceremonies and practices are intricately tied to the Rara, and I observed a sexuality and perverse sort of spirit in the manner in which the women and men danced as they slowly shuffled by the campus on their way to Chambrun. It was fascinating and disturbing at the same time.

December is known as the season when people renew their contract with Satan. I am not sure what exactly that means, but Pastor Pierre and others have shared how sacrifices and voodoo ceremonies are at their peak during the season leading to Christmas. Some say that children even go missing during this time in the more rural areas as human sacrifices still take place on the island.

And then there are the previous stories I wrote already. "The Man with No Face" is an explanation for how Pastor's truck ended up in the ditch (see previous chapter by the same title). When Jocelyn died, our security guard written about in "Lightning Strikes," the people say that one of the witchdoctors "didn't mean for things to go that far." They attribute his death not to a natural phenomenon, a freak accident, but to the direct work of spiritual forces conjured by a witchdoctor.

There was a young Haitian who grew up in Oakland, California. He was here on campus with another ministry that was visiting. I was giving them a tour, and when I learned that he was living here in Haiti (he had lost a son in the earthquake actually) and that his grandfather was a voodoo priest, I decided to see what he thought about the explanation of Jocelyn's death being a result of voodoo. Without hesitation, he knew that it was. Unequivocally yes! He went on to say that it revealed that Jocelyn was not a true follower of Christ. If he was a true follower of Christ, than voodoo would have no power over him. It cannot do anything to you. But if you are not, then voodoo can have great power. I asked him just to be clear, "so there is NO WAY it was a freak act of nature." It seemed as if that was not even a possibility in his mind.

My Posture

What is interesting to me is that many North Americans come to Haiti and have no room for the possibility of the spiritual realities that are simply accepted here. I mentioned earlier that I read a book by Tim Schwartz titled *Travesty in Haiti*. In the second chapter of his book, he writes how he moves in with the local witchdoctor in the village so he will no longer be bothered by the constant requests of the community, and also where the mosquitos do not bite him. They bite him everywhere else in the village, to great annoyance, but as long as he is in the house of this witchdoctor, they do not bite. What is most telling is he can offer no explanation for this. As an anthropologist trained in how to observe and record data, he sees and knows the truth of this reality, but he cannot offer an explanation as to why this is the case. His worldview doesn't have space for an explanation. To a Haitian, the answer is simple: voodoo[2].

My own posture toward voodoo has evolved over the year. When I first arrived in Haiti, I was mostly naïve (and largely still am) to the pervasiveness of voodoo belief and practice in this culture. I became more aware as the year went on, but mostly I just ignored it. As a Christian, I too claim the power of Jesus Christ on my life and believe we have every power over any other powers. But as I sit here and think back on my year, the power and influence of voodoo is pervasive. I really cannot ignore it, as much as I try.

The second thought that comes to mind in regards to my posture is the importance of prayer. Spiritual realities are discerned spiritually. You cannot discern whether an illness or something is caused by a spiritual reality by trying to observe in the physical world. The Bible describes a healing of a man suffering from seizures, what we know today as physical disorder, but Jesus rebukes a demon and the man is healed (Matt 17:15-18). There were many times when myself or others on our team were led to pray for specific things at specific times. Was this the power of the Holy Spirit at work, helping direct and lead us? I hope and believe so.

Another time I remember being invited to pray. I was picking Gestin, our community liaison, up from Trou Caiman, a village where we rent some property and do various ministry activities. He was there meeting with the people, doing Bible teaching and praying with folks. He invited me to pray with two people from the community he had been meeting with. One was suffering from an illness of some sort, the other was renouncing voodoo— at least that was what I gathered. After we prayed with them, we went behind the tent where we were meeting and prayed over the voodoo fetish they were giving up, and then lit it on fire and walked away.

If I was staying in Haiti longer, I would be more intentional in how I pray and in the ways I engage with the culture on this topic. I believe as an

---

[2] To me, it just confirms that mosquitos are in fact from the devil.

American, there are parts of my worldview that need to shift to make room for spiritual realities in a different way than what my American culture typically offers. At the same time, there are probably ways in which Haitians need to be re-envisioned to the natural systems and processes of the world. All of us need more awareness of the power Jesus Christ has over every other power.

Ronaldo

Ronaldo is one of my favorite young men from our children's home. He is the oldest boy currently in our home, and often is looking out for the younger kids. He is the son of a witchdoctor and used to dream about being a witchdoctor himself. He saw the power and fear that his father commanded and wanted that as well. One day Ronaldo got sick and an American doctor who was here took care of him and nurtured him back to health. The care and compassion this doctor showed re-oriented Ronaldo's worldview. Instead of wanting to be a witchdoctor or voodoo priest like his father, he wants to be a medical doctor and help people get well with love and compassion. To me, this is one practical working out of the power of Christ over the power of voodoo, and a fulfillment of the purpose for NVM. Ronaldo is becoming who God has made him to be, a person of love and compassion, not a person of control and fear.

14 WHERE CAN I GO?

One time when Jesus was really starting to get popular and the crowds following him were particularly large, he gave a very difficult teaching. The story is found in John 6:1-71 and it is fascinating. Go read it. After giving this teaching, many of his disciples turned away and never followed him again. And just as everyone else has left, he turns to the twelve and asks them if they want to leave as well.

Okay, pause. Let's review. Right near the start of Jesus' ministry, just as momentum is building, the healings have been happening, the people are wowed by his wisdom and understanding, Jesus gives an extremely confusing and difficult teaching, one that is so challenging that most everyone leaves and deserts him. And instead of saying some encouraging and motivational words to his followers, something to re-energize them and reassure them, he looks to them almost as if he expects them to turn tail and run. Interesting ministry growth strategy, Jesus.

Simon Peter steps up to speak on behalf of the rest:

Simon Peter answered him, "Lord, to whom shall we go? You have the words of eternal life. We believe and know that you are the Holy One of God." (John 6:68-69).

I am not sure what led Peter to make such a reply, or what it took after seeing person upon person turn their shoulder and walk away, for them to stay. I am not sure how big the temptation was for them to go back to what they were doing before. But they remained resolute and stood by Jesus. And they did so probably only half-realizing the cost of following him, a cost so great that all but one would pay with their life. Perhaps they were focused on the rewards, the promise of eternal life, or the proximity of relationship to Jesus.

Whatever the case, it seems that following Jesus is promised to be really, really hard.

Children

Living in Haiti is hard and can be especially hard if you are a child. Too many times I have witnessed this firsthand. In the States, if a child is born prematurely, there are all kinds of things medical professionals can do to help give the child a shot at a healthy life through medicines, machines, education and expertise that are all readily available. Here, there is little that can be done. We had a young baby come in that was born ten weeks early. It easily fit in the palm of my hand. It had just been born a few hours earlier in the hospital, and we urged the mother to try and feed the child. She didn't want to because she had not bathed yet. We didn't understand why bathing was important in this moment. We told her if she didn't feed this child, it was going to die. The mother just kept saying how small the baby was. They left the clinic and later that night, the baby died.

Even children who are born healthy face a hard road. One out of eight children will die before the age of five in Haiti. This is the highest mortality rate among children in the Western Hemisphere. Malnutrition, neglect, even ignorance are often the culprits. The situations that I find are really tough are when such easily preventable things take a young child's life, like diarrhea or malaria. We see many babies in the clinic. It is hard to forget their faces, like the two young twin brothers that were struggling, and a few weeks later, one returns with his mother, the other no longer of this world.

We had a young lady in the clinic who was 100 years old. The nurses took special care to tell her she was beautiful and get to know this precious lady. Living 100 years anywhere is impressive. Living 100 years in Haiti is almost unheard of. During this woman's lifetime, she had given birth to twenty-one children. Of those twenty-one, only seven survived. She had given birth to and buried fourteen babies.

Only July 7, 2011, word came to us that a three-year-old child was thrown in the latrine down in Chambrun. Someone pulled the young child out and cleaned her up. The story goes that the husband left the mother for another woman and the mother no longer wanted the child, so she put her where the rest of the waste goes and took off. The community knew the child and knew there was an aunt over in Croix-des-Bouquets, so they were going to take the child there to see if the aunt could look after her.

On average, every week the staff here at NVM are offered children. Often a parent's emotional, spiritual and physical resources are so depleted in their minds, it is easier to give up the child. Our nurses are often offered a sick child in the clinic. After church one day, Shelli was asked to please take a child back to the States with her when she goes. At a mobile medical clinic, a parent asks if we would please take care of their child as they are unable to do it any longer. It happens time and time again.

One day, while walking through an IDP camp, we encountered three really tough stories right in a row. A mother had a child suffer a head injury that physically disabled the child in the earthquake and now has to take care of her child's physical needs all day. She said, "I am a slave to my child" in her desperation.

We walked up the way just a bit to discover a young child, between the age of two and three, left alone in one of the donated tents NVM provided. The inside of the tent had to be well over 100 degrees, and the parents had left the child laying there as they were off working, doing laundry, or whatever it is they needed to do.

And then there was Edland.

Edland started following our group part-way into the camp. She said in Creole, "I want to go with you" and seemed intent to do so. She followed us along throughout the entire camp. As it got close to time to leave, we started to ask more about this little three-year-old. Word came to us that she lived alone. She was a feral child of sorts, roaming the camp begging for food, sleeping where she lied. When we inquired about her parents, it was a similar story to one we have heard so many times before. The father was with another woman who did not want her, and the mother had taken off to another part of the country. She was left to fend for herself in the camp. As we got in our truck to leave, little Edland chased after us, begging to go with us. It was an image those of us who were in that group will not forget.

Near Miss

Shelli and my low point of the year came on April 5, 2011. We had been in country almost four months exactly, had recently moved out of our tent, and were soon to have our new quarters fully up and operational. I was working in the office, and Shelli was in the dorm preparing beds for a team that was arriving later that day. Sitota was doing one of his favorite activities, which is sweeping. He was next to the washing machines outside, and Wadlaine and a few others were watching. Suddenly, Sitota grabbed a spoon with peanut butter from someone and took off across the parking lot. As he was running, he actually tripped and fell face down. Right at the very same moment, Walton, one of our drivers was backing up the old Toyota pick-up truck at a fairly quick rate of speed. Everyone started yelling as it was clear that Walton did not see Sitota in his path. He stopped just short of running over our son with the rear wheel parked right on Sitota's right foot. Sitota immediately started screaming and was very scared. They quickly moved the truck forward, scooped him up and rushed him into the clinic to be checked out by the doctor.

Neither Shelli nor I saw the near miss. When I got word that Sitota was in an accident, I rushed to the clinic and found that Shelli had arrived just ahead of me. The report Shelli got was that Sitota was hit by a truck and in the clinic, so needless to say, she was in quite a panic. The doctor stripped him down to his diaper and had already checked him out. The good news is that physically Sitota was totally fine. He was more scared by how frightened everyone else was around him, and of course the giant truck parked on his foot probably had something to do with it.

This incident hit us like a ton of bricks. Nothing in this world is more precious to us than our children, and this accident could have been very serious. It was only by God's grace that it was not more serious. Emotionally, this was the straw that broke the proverbial camel's back. One look at Shelli, and I could tell something had broken within her and was not going to be easily repaired. For one, she is not much of a crier, and she couldn't stop crying. I was trying to be strong, but it was downright scary.

Two days later Shelli and the kids were on a plane to be with her parents in Orlando for two weeks. Her parents took great care of everyone and helped refuel the emotional storage tanks. I worked for another week to help get some critical projects finished up, and then I joined them.

Pain and Suffering

I in no way want to suggest I have a deep insight into suffering and pain. There are many more people who have gone before me, and certainly those who will come after me, who have seen and experienced far more pain and suffering than I have. And a result of their experience, and due to being far smarter than me, they have great insights and wisdom to share on the nature of it. I only mean to offer my simple thoughts from my limited experience of living here in Haiti.

Many people will write us an e-mail, and they say things that are aimed at being encouraging. And they are encouraging! Things like "you guys are so inspirational" or "I can't imagine!" or "I don't know how you do it." But I think of these statements, considering the source from which they come, as also sometimes a "thank-you for doing what I cannot do." They are expressions to state that what they think we are doing is hard and to keep going. It is almost as if they are trying to say we are doing something special. But that's the thing about it. I don't feel like we are doing anything special. We are just doing what God has led us to do. Maybe it is special, but I'm no one special for doing it.

And I guess it is hard. And yet I contrast my situation with the words of Jesus in Matthew 11:28-30:

"Come to me, all you who are weary and burdened, and I will give you rest. Take my yoke upon you and learn from me, for I am gentle and humble in heart, and you will find rest for your souls. For my yoke is easy and my burden is light."

Really? Your burden is light? Compared to what?

I know it wasn't light for Paul, but he actually boasted of all the things he suffered. He does so in 2 Corinthians 11 and 12. Read the passage, it is really quite remarkable all the things that Paul has suffered. Stoning, shipwrecked three times, five times whipped, beaten with a rod, and the list goes on. Yet he boasts because the things he suffered serve to reveal God's power and mission in the world. Paul claimed to be shackled to Christ, such that it was no longer he who lived. It was no longer his will for things, but as much as possible, it was Christ who lives in him.

Galatians 2:20: "I have been crucified with Christ and I no longer live, but Christ lives in me. The life I live in the body, I live by faith in the Son of God, who loved me and gave himself for me."

So pain and suffering, well, that is for Christ's glory.

Pastor Pierre has suffered greatly for his decision to follow the Spirit of God to be hope and light in Haiti. He has suffered attempted kidnappings of his children, direct threats of violence, hunger and sleeplessness, the death of all his classmates, his best friends, and too many others in the earthquake. He has suffered from family pressures, from rumors, and countless other ways. And yet, he seems to equate all this suffering like Paul does, for Christ's glory.

Strangely, pain and suffering is taking on a new light to my dull mind here in Haiti. Maybe it is because I am surrounded by so much struggle daily in my Haitian brother's and sister's daily lives. Maybe it is because this has been one of the toughest years of my life. Whatever the reason, there is a shift taking place. While pain and suffering were once things to be feared and avoided, they are now viewed as opportunity. We get the privilege (not punishment) of entering into other's pain in order to (to borrow from NVM) shine light in the darkness, in order to turn hopelessness into the hope of eternal life. By choosing Christ, we actually choose a great paradox. We may have trouble in this world, but Jesus has overcome the world (John 16:33).

And knowing Jesus and being a conduit for His work...there is no comparison for finding meaning in life.

15 DO THE POOR KNOW YOU BY NAME?

Onaville

There is a community that has developed since the earthquake just a couple of miles from our campus. If you stand on the roof of one of our buildings, you can see it clearly on the hillside to the west. It is actually a cluster of communities going by different names, but they all have in common the fact that their inhabitants are internally displaced people. It is a large IDP camp.

There are many large NGOs who are doing various work out there including building small homes, building a school, providing security through the UN and Haitian police outposts, and providing water in giant bladders. NVM has rights to some property pretty far up the hill in an area called Onaville. O-N-A is sort of like Haiti's version of social security, and there is actually a retirement community of homes built at the foot of the mountain that were constructed under President Aristide that people who paid into ONA could elect to rent in their retirement. We were in there once and only eight of the ninety-two units were rented.

We have a tent on the property and are beginning to build relationships with the community. To date, we have taken vision clinics, medical clinics, and dental clinics up there. The Jesus Film Project has probably done the most work in showing the Jesus Film and building relationships with local leaders. The community is now begging us to start a church there, and we are taking steps to do it.

I got in the habit of trying to take teams to Onaville towards the end of their time in Haiti. Our tour would start in another community we are working in called Trou Caiman, and then to Onaville for a hike and a short talk. We would end our time up the road a bit further at a mass grave site where hundreds of thousands of people who perished in Port-au-Prince from the earthquake are buried. It is at Onaville where I would pray that the Spirit of God would meet us in a powerful way, and God often did.

To the Top of the Mountain

When we would pull off the paved road and head into Onaville, it was always a bumpy ride. I'll try to take you there with me: imagine going from a smooth surface onto an uneven, rocky dirt road. We pass through a new neighborhood still under construction. Latrines line the boundaries with solar powered security lights overhead. The homes are small, about twenty feet by forty feet, and built closely together. Picture a work shed in the back of a typical American home. They are simple, one room structures without electricity, water, kitchens or bathrooms. Every time I drive through, I wonder with nervousness how they will hold up in a hurricane.

There are also many tent structures scattered around the rows of newly built homes. Some are more sophisticated than others, and there are a few people who have started building more permanent homes with concrete. This settlement is here to stay.

We pass a brand new school. It is a beautiful complex, full of many buildings, newly opened, painted a bright yellow with white accents. You can tell it was built by an American NGO, as there is a basketball court right in the middle of the courtyard. I wonder how long it will take the students to turn the court into a pitch for playing soccer.

After we pass through a dry riverbed, one that is steep enough to make my passengers worry about scraping the front bumper (we don't), we pass one of the only wells I have seen in the community. People walk from all over to get their water at this well. Just a few hundred more yards, and we arrive at our little fenced-in property. Just the drive in usually has great impact for our teams, most who have never seen poverty like they are surrounded by here.

There is a small hill/mountain behind our property. It takes about fifteen minutes to walk to the top, just enough of a hike to feel it in your lungs if you walk at a decent pace. Just about every team member is able to do the short walk, and the view from there stretches from the ocean to the west near Port-au-Prince all the way to the Dominican Republic to the east. You can clearly see the campus of NVM, and you can see the thousands and thousands of tents and homes below us. With the mountains in the background, the sun high in the sky, it is a beautiful, sacred, hopeful place to stand.

Do the Poor Know You by Name?

After everyone has had a chance to catch their breath, drink a little water, maybe snap a few pictures, I pull everyone in close. If it is windy, which it often is, I check to make sure everyone can hear me clearly. And then   I   start   in   with   my   message:

I brought you up here today to ask you a question. It is late in the week, you have by this time met many Haitians, hopefully made some new friends, experienced much of the beauty and great need that is found here. And it is now that I want to ask you a question...and it is a question that I hope the Holy Spirit sears on your heart, a question that haunts your mind long after you leave Haiti and return home. I have been praying that God would do this. I can't make it happen, all I can do is ask the question and it is up to you and the Holy Spirit what you do with it.

I like to really work up the expectation in the first few moments before I ask the question. I usually try and leave long pauses between my statements so as to increase the expectation.

The question is this: Do the poor know you by name? Do the poor...know YOU...by name?

Now this is a really, really important question. And it is important for a number of reasons. And frankly, it really is not even my questions to start with. I stole it, and basically re-phrased it from Jesus. The story is found in Matthew 25:31-46[3]

---

[3] Matthew 25:31-46 "When the Son of Man comes in his glory, and all the angels with him, he will sit on his throne in heavenly glory. 32 All the nations will be gathered before him, and he will separate the people one from another as a shepherd separates the sheep from the goats. 33 He will put the sheep on his right and the goats on his left. 34 "Then the King will say to those on his right, 'Come, you who are blessed by my Father; take your inheritance, the kingdom prepared for you since the creation of the world. 35 For I was hungry and you gave me something to eat, I was thirsty and you gave me something to drink, I was a stranger and you invited me in, 36 I needed clothes and you clothed me, I was sick and you looked after me, I was in prison and you came to visit me.' 37 "Then the righteous will answer him, 'Lord, when did we see you hungry and feed you, or thirsty and give you something to drink? 38 When did we see you a stranger and invite you in, or needing clothes and clothe you? 39 When did we see you sick or in prison and go to visit you?' 40 "The King will reply, 'I tell you the truth, whatever you did for one of the least of these brothers of mine, you did for me.' 41 "Then he will say to those on his left, 'Depart from me, you who are cursed, into the eternal fire prepared for the devil and his angels. 42 For I was hungry and you gave me nothing to eat, I was thirsty and you gave me nothing to drink, 43 I was a stranger and you did not invite me in, I needed clothes and you did not clothe me, I was sick and in prison and you did not look after me.' 44 "They also will answer, 'Lord, when did we see you hungry or thirsty or a stranger or needing clothes or sick or in prison, and did not help you?' 45 "He will reply, 'I tell you the

Sheep and Goats.

I don't quote the text word for word. I give them the "Aaron paraphrase" version, which hopefully has more impact as it is coming from my heart rather than reading directly out of the book. I actually picture myself teaching as Jesus did, on the side of a mountain, the wind in his face, no sound projection equipment to amplify his voice. I am not always aware if God is actually working in hearts and minds, but by faith I believe he is working.

So here is the scene. At the end of time, all the people from every nation are brought before the king and all his angels. It is clearly implied that Jesus is the king, and every type of person is included...American, Asian, European, Haitian...everyone is included. And everyone is divided into one of two groups...you are either a sheep or a goat. If you have been paying attention this week, you probably have seen plenty of sheep and goats. The sheep are put on the right, and the goats on the left.

The king next turns to the sheep and says, "You are blessed! Thank you for taking care of me. When I was hungry, you fed me, when I was thirsty, you gave me something to drink. When I was a stranger or homeless, you took me in, when I was naked you clothed me, when I was sick or in prison, you came to visit me."

And of course, the sheep are shocked. "When did we see you Jesus and do all these things? We don't remember seeing you!"

And then this is the really profound part. Jesus says to them, "Whatever you did to the least of these brothers or sisters of mine, you did to me."

Whoa. This is unbelievable. Jesus in this moment identifies himself as actually being found in those we would consider the "least of these" in the world. And so a great secret is revealed. No doubt God is in the places where you come from...he is in your suburban/rural/urban/middle class/wealthy/North American (insert relevant location based on team) neighborhoods from which you come. But if you want to be sure and find Jesus, he will be found in the least of these in the world. Have you met Jesus this week? My guess is that you have had opportunity if you have been paying attention.

And it is really, really important to meet Jesus here. Because next he turns to those on his left and says "Cursed are you...goats. I was hungry, and you ignored me, I was thirsty and you walked right by. I was without a home and you told me to get a job, I was a stranger and you were too afraid of me to invite me in, I was sick or in prison and you told me I was getting what I deserved."

I often try and contemporize the reasons why we often do not engage with the least of these in the world. Certainly there are many reasons, and I

truth, whatever you did not do for one of the least of these, you did not do for me.'
46 "Then they will go away to eternal punishment, but the righteous to eternal life."

actually feel some sympathy for the goats based on their reaction.

And of course the goats are just as shocked as the sheep. They have the same reaction! "Jesus, when did we see you hungry and ignore you? When did we see you thirsty? When were you at our door and we didn't let you in? If we had known it was you, the king, we would have visited you in prison or in the hospital? When did we see you?"

And again, Jesus will reply, "Whatever you did NOT do for these brothers and sisters of mine, you did not do for me."

This is really, really important. In fact, this is the only place in scripture that I know of where Jesus actually sends someone to hell. There are many places where Jesus warns people that they are in danger of the fires of hell or says "watch out!," but in this story the goats are actually sent away.

Jesus Cared for, Jesus is Known

So why is it so important? Well, on the one hand, the poor in the world often need what you have. They need the love of Jesus, they need good news. They need clothes, or food, or the belief that they have value. Poverty is multi-faceted; it is not simply an economic issue. And you in the world who have been given so much also have a great responsibility to love and care for those who have little. Jesus gets taken care of and his needs get met in this world when you extend yourself and give. This is important for the poor who need what you have to offer.

But it is also just as important, I would wager even more important, that you get to know Jesus in the lives of those with great need. It is far more important because in the context of this story, it determines whether you are a sheep or a goat, and whether you go to a place of inheritance, a Kingdom prepared by God, or to hell. And so I come to the question…do the poor know you...do they know Brian, Lisa, Annie, David (I always name people who are standing there listening as much as possible) by name?

Framing the question as I do demands a relational proximity.

Not that they know your dollars that you gave anonymously through an organization, but do they know you. Personally. Have you gotten close enough to allow the poor to know you by name? Do you know anyone who is in the situation Jesus describes by name? Do the poor know YOU, by name?

When you go home, will you find Jesus in the least of these in your own community? No matter where you come from, they are there. You may have to look harder than you do in Haiti, but they are there. You can certainly stay engaged here in Haiti…there are lots of ways to do that, but I pray that you do meet Jesus somewhere.

Will you be a sheep or a goat? Have you met Jesus in the least of these? Do the poor know you by name?

My Question

The challenge that I put to teams has now become my own. At the writing of this chapter, I am a few weeks from returning from Haiti back to Hamilton County, Indiana. Where I live now is considered the poorest country in the Western Hemisphere. It is a place where I know many who are poor in the world by first name. The community I return to in Indiana is one of the wealthiest counties in probably the wealthiest country to ever exist in the history of humanity. Will the poor in Haiti continue to know me by name? Will I continue to participate in the alleviation of poverty here? Will I continue to be known by name, and know those in this community by name?

And now there is a new set of questions as well. Will the poor in my own community, a community in which those who are poor are increasing in number quickly, will they know my name? Yes, Hamilton County is wealthy, but there is a quickly growing population of those that can't meet their basic needs right in my own backyard. It is easier to find folks in Indianapolis, and I have partners that help me engage and build relationships there. But what about Hamilton County? Can I make my way to know those in my neighborhoods, especially when it seems the culture wants to keep them hidden? I know it is a question I am wrestling with just as I put it to the teams...will the poor know me by name? It is critically important that I meet Jesus!

I also return to my role as an Associate Pastor at a large church hoping to create a sense of urgency in the unaware people around me. The book I recommended most this year to people coming to engage in ministry in Haiti, particularly those who come for more than just a week or come back multiple times, is titled When Helping Hurts: How to Alleviate Poverty without Hurting the Poor...and Yourself (by Steve Corbett and Brian Fikkert). From their introduction, page 28:

North American Christians are simply not doing enough. We are the richest people ever to walk the face of the earth. Period. Yet, most of us live as though there is nothing terribly wrong in the world. We attend our kids' soccer games, pursue our careers, and take beach vacations while 40 percent of the world's inhabitants struggle just to eat every day. And in our own backyards, the homeless, those residing in ghettos, and a wave of immigrants live in a world outside the economic and social mainstream of North America. We do not necessarily need to feel guilty about our wealth. But we do need to get up every morning with a deep sense that something is terribly wrong with the world and yearn to strive to do something about it. There is simply not enough yearning and striving going on.

It is my hope to continue to make people aware so that the Kingdom

Jesus spoke about can come fully to earth, just as it is in Heaven. In the Spirit of Nehemiah, there are walls to be rebuilt and a people to reestablish, the people of God need to come into their own. And God's heart is that all people would enter into his presence, not just sometime off in the future in eternity, but today…now.

And the gates of hell will not prevail.

There is light for those in darkness, there is hope for the hopeless, there is eternal life that is offered rather than death.

Come Lord Jesus.

16 HOME

December 19, 2011

It has been almost five weeks since I stepped off the plane at the Indianapolis airport. I have been very intentional about waiting until now to finish up this project. I have attempted to live in the present the last few weeks, attempting to withhold evaluations or judgments of the people or things around me. I was told that the transition home could be challenging. The cultural realities of rural Haiti and suburban Indianapolis are very, very different, and in many ways obvious. But then again, some things are not so different, and some things are very subtle. When people ask me how I am doing, my most common reply is "I'm working on it."

Adjustments

My kids have done well, although it has taken longer for them to adjust then I expected. I am not sure where my expectations came from that assumed that they would settle quickly back into life and routines here. Maybe it is because we have been toting our kids along with us all over the place for many years. Maybe it was because I remember living in our home for 10 years prior to Haiti, forgetting that my oldest is only 8. Our son, Sitota, did not remember living in our home. The first week he kept saying "I want to go home." I would remind him that "we are home buddy" and he would reply, "Nooooo, my home in Haiti." Most nights the first weeks I would wake up in the morning to find him snuggled in between Shelli and I in our king-size bed. Thankfully our bed is much bigger than in Haiti and I would not even notice he found his way in until I woke up the next morning!

I have probably been most aware of the changes through attempting to parent Isabel, my oldest. We waited two weeks before we started school, and those weeks were filled with buying clothes, school supplies, and Thanksgiving festivities. Our kids had lived a year in a Caribbean climate so the one pair of crocs they owned was just not going to be sufficient for the up and coming Indiana winter. When Isabel finally started school, she was completely exhausted after her first day. She struggled to do a math assignment she had already finished in Haiti. This continued for the next couple of weeks as homework she easily did in 15 or 20 minutes would take her more than an hour, usually through tears and the supportive presence of Mom or Dad sitting closely next to her.

Our support has been nothing short of humbling and frankly, almost overwhelming at times. Our house was fully stocked with meals in the fridge and freezer, our house was clean, there were fresh flowers on the island, gift cards for buying our kids clothes, for groceries, for any number of things. It seemed like everywhere we went someone was saying "welcome home" and "it is so good to have you back!" The kids were provided brand new winter coats, hats, and gloves, all of such high quality that will actually grow with them and last more than one year.

Choices

The first week I was back at work, a group of us went out to lunch. There were eight of us sitting around the table and I was getting overwhelmed by the menu. There were so many options for lunch! Not only did they have everything on the menu (in Haiti, often they only have a couple of things available even if they have a dozen things listed on the menu), but each person was able to order what they wanted in their own special way. Everyone seemed to want their beverage a particular way…half diet, half regular for this guy, water with lemon slice for the next lady…and then came the food orders. There were probably an unlimited number of options for what you can order, what you can hold, what you can add, and cooked just the way you like.

The number of choices that are thrown out me each day has been a struggle. In rural Haiti, there is not the constant demand for my attention by this advertisement, or the next social network site on my computer, or the next retail store advertising the next greatest thing to make my life easier. Most days I simply needed to remember to bring my sunglasses so as not to spend the day squinting under the gorgeous sunshine.

I believe in freedom. Choices are a good thing, and they matter a lot. But I find myself wondering at how many choices a person really needs. It seems I have entered the land of choice, looking for someone to still some of the noise so I can simply enjoy what I have, which is so much more than I need.

Thoughts of Haiti

Within the first week of being home, we got word that there was a short-term team that was in Haiti at a partner ministry of NVM. I actually knew some of the pastors that were on the team as we had worked with them on a regional event together. Apparently a group of Haitian men broke into the dorm where they were staying seeking to rob them. Shots were fired and four people were injured. Thankfully no one was seriously injured and they were all flown out of Haiti on a private plane and returned safely to the US. Just one week prior, Shelli and I stood in the dorm where the break-in and shooting occurred. We immediately thought of NVM and how if it happened at this ministry, then it could happen at NVM.

Pastor assured everyone that our security was a little better than our partner, and that we would be taking additional steps to insure we were taking every precaution. He also indicated his suspicion that it was probably an inside job of some kind. Someone who knew a lot about the ministry had to be involved the way they intentionally sought out the American team. Thankfully, they were caught a few weeks later. The police in Haiti are cracking down on crime in a big way currently.

Just this past Friday my son woke up from his nap with a huge lump on the left side of his neck and swelling in his face. He started running a fever the night before, but had not had other symptoms of sickness. Shelli immediately recognized there was a problem and put him in the car. After stopping by the church to show me, we decided we should go to the Emergency Room. It seems Sitota acquired a bacterial infection in his lymph nodes. The concern was that they could abscess which would require surgery, or they could become septic which could be very serious. He was transitioned to the Peyton Manning Children's hospital for an inpatient stay and was treated with IV antibiotics every 6 hours until he was released Sunday to continue oral antibiotics at home.

God was extremely gracious to us. Sitota is a very healthy boy. He has never had so much as a cold since the first day we have had him. If this infection had developed in Haiti, it could have been very, very serious as IV antibiotics can be very difficult to find. The CT scan he received to discover how infected the lymph nodes were would have been nearly impossible. If the infection had developed between the 15th when we came home and the first of December, we would have been without health insurance.

Again, our community has been tremendously supportive. Back in Haiti, we got word that Mica, Louna, Wadlaine, and Eliana saw a picture of Sitota on one of the nurses Facebook pages and wanted us to know they were praying for him. To know our friends, back in their mud huts, were praying was so amazing.

Life is so fragile. We have such an illusion of control back here in the states. In Haiti, you are so dependent, all the time, on God and on others. You are dependent here too, but the illusion is that you can control things. I feel for the team that was injured and am thankful that God protected them. I pray it does not dissuade people from stepping out in faith and going where God is leading them in the future. I also feel for every mother in Haiti that feels so helpless to care for their child when disease comes. I felt completely helpless and we had excellent care! Through it all, we are in God's hands.

It is Not Fair

I say to my kids when they yell "it's not fair" that "life is not fair. Sorry."

It really isn't. And I get mad when it is not fair against me. For some reason, maybe it was the way I was raised, believing that life is what you make it and that I have every opportunity in life just so long as I work hard and apply myself. I don't seem to mind so much when it is not fair in my favor. I am still struggling with much of the unfairness to life. Fifi is still in Haiti, waiting for the President to sign her adoption papers so she can come home to Indiana. She has waited three months for this signature now, and we are still counting. This just doesn't seem fair.

My friend Clerice works so hard to get ahead in life, helping support and take care of his two sisters, brother, Mom, and young son back home. Through his relationships at NVM, he has found a sponsor in the United States to help him go to school. Clerice is the type of guy who will go, get a great education, come back and be a part of the solution for Haiti. Since coming home, Clerice was denied his Visa to the US for a second time. Apparently they don't believe someone would help pay for his school in the states, or something like that. All Clerice wants is an opportunity. At NVM he has worked as a translator, greatly improving his already very good English, leading our Children's church, learning to operate heavy equipment, learning any and everything he can. And this has been awesome…but he is still limited and somewhat stuck until a door opens that he can walk through. Why do the doors keep shutting for Clerice when they seem to swing wide open for others?

I took a phone call from a good friend today. Her young child has been sick, throwing up and battling dehydration. Her husband has also been battling illness for the last five or six weeks. He is prone to lung infections, pneumonia and bronchitis. My friend was extremely tired from caring for sick family members, including a struggling mother-in-law, all while trying to work and get some sleep herself. She probably had not slept more than five hours in a row for the last two weeks.

I listened with genuine compassion and empathy. I know what it is like to be up late at night with sick kids or a sick spouse. I know what it is like to have to work hard in the midst of little sleep. And I was struck by how hard it really is. I nearly teared up myself as I listened to my friend on the other end start to let some of the emotion out that she has been keeping in for a long time. And yet I contrast it to what I know of life in Haiti. So many Moms are completely on their own, without a spouse. When their child is sick, there is little or no access to doctors that prescribe Pedialyte and ask you to follow up in two days. And what is even more difficult is that my friend needs compassion just as much as a mother in Haiti. How do I reconcile these two worlds, worlds where capacities are so very different?

Coming Home

Shelli and I know when we are home. It has been when we were sitting around with our small group the first time we arrived back. We have been doing life with three couples for many years. Two of the couples we have met with weekly for nearly twelve years. The other couple joined the group three or four years ago and are our next door neighbors. When our kids are all playing together and we are being picked on as if we never left, this is when we know we are home.

Or the first weekend we went out with two other couples that we know and love and do life with. They took us to dinner, allowed us space to share, got ridiculous and caused uncontrollable fits of laughter. Again, when we are with these friends, we know we are home as we are completely accepted and loved, not for being special or being missionaries, but for just being ourselves.

When we go to our jobs and find people who have been waiting for us to come back, who are excited to have us do the things we love to do again, we know we are home. Sure, part of being home is our house and our physical location, but it seems home is more and more the relationships that will last into eternity. There is one sense where home is not fully realized as we long for the intimacy with our creator that can only be found after we die. But there is another sense that home is the many relationships that help define who we are. Home is in Haiti, it is in Ohio where many of our extended family live, it is in Florida where Shelli's parents take such good care of us, and it is in Indiana where the majority of our community live.

It is good to be home.

Conclusions

There are three themes or threads that I want to reflect upon to finish this project. First is the idea that every person, no matter how young or old, has the opportunity to be involved in the on-going work of God in the world in a place that really matters. I will call it the front lines of ministries. I call it the front lines because this is often the place where darkness meets light, where hopelessness is replaced with hope. It is the place where God's

Kingdom breaks in and the powers of darkness lose their power. It is a dangerous place, often a place of great need. In Haiti, there is a lot of front line work that is going on all around. There is plenty of front line work back here in my suburban context as well, but it is tougher to find sometimes. Regardless, I think everyone can and needs to be involved.

Not everyone will go to Haiti. I recognize that a family of five moving to Haiti is very unique, certainly not for everyone. But in today's world, there are so many ways to be in relationship with someone who has great need. If not directly through volunteering with a local ministry or going on a short-term trip, then indirectly through a relationship with someone who is on the front lines of ministry. Our family could flat out not have gone with the support of the community around us. We could not have gone, and we could not have survived had we gotten there, without the support of others. And every victory, every success, every person who started a relationship with Jesus Christ, every person who was baptized, every new church we helped start, every person we fed or clothed, or every child who received health care because we were in Haiti is not only the fruit or our faithfulness, but is the fruit of each and every person who participated with us.

And we know how important it is to meet Jesus and know him in the face of the least of these (see Do the Poor Know You by Name). Get involved in some way. The poor in the world, the hopeless, the ones with no food or clothes, they desperately need what you have in excess. And you desperately need what they have to offer as well.

A second theme I have discovered in this year speaks to our identity as followers of Jesus Christ. I was recently reminded of the story of Jacob wrestling with God all night (Genesis 32:24-32) and not letting him go until he was blessed. The blessing came in the form of a new name, "Israel" which means "he wrestles with God." This became the name of the entire nation and still is to this day. The people of God are the ones who "wrestle with God."

As followers of Christ, we are invited into a living relationship with God in which we are permitted to "wrestle" with God. Over this year, I saw many hard things that left me filled with doubt, fear, pain, and anger. But as I took them to God and began to wrestle with them, I saw faith begin to replace doubt, seeing that God cares so much more than I do. I saw fear give way to courage and boldness. I saw pain transformed into a character that extends compassion to others. I saw anger give way to peace as I learn to trust God who has better plans than I can come up with on my own.

This process by no means is an easy one at every moment. Jacob left with his hip wrenched. Ouch! I still am struggling with God on many things, most notably Fifi's adoption and lack of progress. If we are commanded to care for widows and orphans, and we are doing just that, why can't God exercise a little sovereignty and help the process move along? The longing of a parents heart who is separated from a child is so heavy to bear. And yet, only as I wrestle with God on the deep injustices I experience, and the pain I bear, and the hardships of the community around me, do I discover who God is in the midst, and his heart and thoughts. And only as I wrestle do find the actions that I must do.

This leads to my last series of thoughts. If you had asked me if God was faithful prior to my year in Haiti, I would have responded with an unequivocal "yes." Of course God is faithful. Even when we are not faithful, God continues to be faithful. I know this to be true in the testimony of Scripture and I know it experientially. There are many ways God has demonstrated his faithfulness to us over the years. I suppose you could say he built our faith in such a way that we were willing to say "YES!" to him when He invited us to spend a year serving in Haiti. Only a demonstration of his faithfulness over the years would have led me to take my family to Haiti as we did.

But to say "God is faithful" today takes on much deeper and profound meaning for me. There is a deep knowing that God is faithful in the face of babies dying from malnutrition or preventable and curable diseases, in the freak accidents that take one man's use of his legs, and the life of another man, or in a culture of voodoo and strange spiritual realities. Saying God is faithful does not mean that things always work out well, or that I will feel happy and good about things at times. It simple means that God will never leave me, or any follower of his. He will always be present with us. And his presence with us makes life bearable once again. It transforms us into the peddlers of hope and light in the world, over and against every power that would say otherwise. And God's faithfulness also offers the hope that all things will be made right in eternity, a hope that does not disappoint.

God is faithful. This alone was worth the entire year.

17 APPENDIX 1

Aubree Dell's version of the Lightning Strike.

From her blog: aubreedell.wordpress.com

Wednesday, September 15th, just three months after our last horrific night at Bernard Mevs (formerly known as Miami Dade Hospital), we were on our way to drop off some donations that Kacie and I had wanted to donate for the past few months. We finally got a truck and the time to go, and I was so excited to travel to the hospital for a positive, exciting reason. We met Rachel when we arrived, a women who works in logistics. She was there the night of Jay's accident. She was amazing and helped get a medivac flight arranged for Jay.

On the way home though I got a feeling deep down inside me. A feeling that is all too familiar to me. I shared my feelings with everyone in the truck that I felt something bad was going to happen soon. Aaron half joking told me to shut up, and not say that. I knocked on some wood, or the plastic panel on our new pick-up truck to not jinx us and did not give it too much thought after that.

Saturday we went to the beach! It was beautiful and amazing! I even bought fresh lobster to bring back and eat! Then when we got home Kacie and Amy whom came to visit for a few days greeted us! Sunday came and went, we played with Rose all day and once again life was good.

Monday morning came and patients greeted me as I tried to make my way to the clinic. Friends telling me they did not get a number to see the doctor and wanted me to fix the problem. I usually hate Mondays around here, because people put their children in my arms and ask for help when I cannot always help them. I have been trying really hard to stick to the "right way" of doing things, which is better for them in the long run.

The men all played a game of soccer that afternoon, but it ended due to a lightning storm and rain. It was a little after six o'clock and we were all eating dinner when we heard the LOUDEST BOOM I have ever heard and felt. The ground shook and I jumped a mile while trying to make a plate of food for the security guards. Adam and Aaron ran outside expecting to see a building on fire, but came back in saying everything looked good. We all turned back to eating when Michel walked casually inside and got Lupson. Next, all the Haitians got up and started nervously chattering. I was unsure what was going on because usually the first thing people do is yell for me when someone is hurt.

Aaron kept asking, "What is wrong? What is going on?" My eyes met Kacie's and we knew something was bad. He heard Gestin was hurt and I immediately took off sprinting out the door behind Kacie. Kacie started running toward Chambrun and I followed behind her, telling Brooke to get Aaron and a truck now. I thought at the time we were running to the village, but as we reached the gate we saw Jocelin, one of the security gaurds. Adam passed us both and reached him first yelling, "Are you ok?" Nothing. We flipped him over and I could feel no pulse. We quickly came to the same conclusion and I started chest compressions while Adam did respirations. We heard some gurgling. I felt ribs crack beneath my fingers as rain pelted our soaking wet bodies. Adam started to cut off his shirt and sack while I still was doing compressions. We started to smell burnt flesh, and could see the burn mark across his chest. More people showed up and we placed oxygen in his nose, put him on a backboard, and headed to Bernard Mevs.

I do not think I can put into words the next 45 minutes, but I will try.

There were 8 bodies in the back of the truck, flying down bumpy Haitian roads. The tailgate was down because the backboard would not have fit with it closed. Rain was pelting our faces and stinging our eyeballs. We were soaking wet. While someone was doing compressions we held on to them with every bit of strength we had in us, stabilizing them and holding them up so they could continue quality chest compressions.

I was performing respirations. Each breath I took, I could taste the brunt flesh that was over taking his body. I tried to stabilize his head so I could give him adequate breaths, but with each bump and turn it became more and more difficult.

After 45 minutes of CPR we were all exhausted. We started encouraging each other and sing that infamous CPR song, "Ah Ah Ah AH, Staying Alive, staying alive…" to help keep the rhythm. When we got to the hospital we immediately got him in and on a bed where Adam and Kacie continued compressions. Leslee and I worked on an IV but could not find a vein. Kacie ended up getting an IV and pushed Epi, but nothing. I grabbed a stool, hitting a doctor in the head so I could relieve Adam from compressions and a couple minutes later a Haitian doctor called it.

And it was over.

Tired and in shock I walked outside to meet my Haitian friends. Ricardo looked at me and I shook my head. All the men with us just looked down and stood there still. I hugged Ricardo who was closer than the others to Jocelin and felt him collapse into me. I kept thinking, stay strong, stay strong. I hugged the rest of the men and went back inside, to find Adam and Kacie cleaning up the body.

It was at this time we realized his cell phone that was in his pocket was completely fried. His zipper on his pants had busted off and the button was burnt and melted. We could see the entrance wound at the top of his shoulder and it must have exited out his left upper leg, because everything was melted to his skin.

The aroma of burnt flesh was potent.

There was another critical patient that was coming in and they asked us to move Jocelin. We loaded him up on a stretcher, placed him in a body bag, and moved him outside around the back of the ER. We put his body close to the wall so the rain would stay off him and his family could come see him.

I stood outside with Leslee, Etienne, and Adam by the back door to the ER. I starred at the same green door I became so familiar with just three months ago. Jay had laid in the bed closest to the door, which was occupied by a patient with a stab wound. I began to flash back to that awful day, but knew I could not go there. It didn't take long and another patient distracted me.

She was in a private room behind me with the door wide open. She was on oxygen (non-rebreather), breathing close to 50 breaths per minute if not more. Her mom walked out and was having dinner, so I sat beside her and asked about her daughter. She had a disease that required the family to wear masks, but the mother could not tell me the name of the disease. I thought, great we are all being exposed out here, but it didn't really matter. I shared with her about the friend we had just lost and she said she was sorry.

The next thing I knew Aaron arrived with the family and a change of warm, dry clothes for us all. The dad was somber as he looked at his son. No one spoke. I felt numb, I kept thinking did this really just happen? We made it home, showered and went to bed.

The next morning I woke up, numb. I went out to find my flip-flops I had lost while running the night before. They were scattered in puddles and when I reached them I looked up and could see three security guards at the gate. I prayed God would not ask me to go out there; I did not want to break down, but knew I had too. I walked up and gave Amos a big hug. Tears quickly fell from his cheeks, I hugged Jean and he began to weep. I felt the Lord whisper pray in my ear. I asked them if I could pray and they all nodded yes. I laid my hands on two of their shoulders and started to pray in Kringlish.

Afterwards, I walked back to the clinic to find Natasha saying we would be closing the clinic for an hour, to have a service for the employees. I sat next to Amos and cried with him all the way through. When it was over I went back to the clinic trying to hold everything together, but my heart hurt so badly.

The next day we celebrated Nathan's birthday.

Friday was Brooke's birthday.

Then the day I really dreaded came. I knew that the funeral service was going to be bad, but I could have never imagined just how crazy it was. I woke up at six to the sound of wailing as people walked from Chambrun. I balled on the floor and thought how am I going to do this? I made it dressed and went over to the church with the American staff. Some of us wore shirts Gestin had made that said, Nou PaP Janm Bliye-w, We will never forget you, with Jocelin's picture on the front.

The church was packed and several people were outside on benches wailing hysterically. I knew over half of the people and it broke my heart to see the community I have come to love and call home hurt. I wept and it was the first time in my life I didn't care if people saw me crying. I don't think I could have held back tears if I really wanted to.

A close friend of mine was helping carry people outside when they became too hysterical. I watched as he would wrestle down women, and thought how can he hold this all together? Shortly he started to get worked up. He yelled for me and I followed him outside. I quickly pulled him away from the chaos and got him a drink of cold water. He told me he was with Jocelin that night. He was suppose to wait for him, but decided to turn back because it was raining. He kept asking me if he did the right thing? I assured him he did nothing wrong and him being their would not have made a difference. We prayed and he was calm. He took my hand and led me back to the church.

When I reached the doors, Jocelin's brother grabbed me and kept saying, "Aubree, what did you do? Where is Jocelin?" He ripped the picture off my shirt and tore it up into pieces. Adam, who was now playing security at the funeral grabbed my hand and pulled me into the church where I was safe. I stood in the corner and tried to listen to the preacher talk about Jocelin's life. However, when people are screaming, wailing, kicking, and constantly being carried out of church it was hard to pay attention. Aaron, Adam, and Nathan stood at the entrance catching people as they tried to dart in.

Women would be in a full sprint, flailing everywhere and one of the men would brace themselves for the impact and carry them back to the bench outside.

It was unreal.

At the end people would come up to me and ask me, why, why Aubree? People in this community look to me for answers, for medical help and expect me to work miracles sometimes. As the casket was being rolled out one of my friends turned to me and yelled Auuuubbbbreeeee as she shrugged her shoulders pointing to the casket. I felt as though I let a community down. I know we gave it our all and did everything we could, and that Jocelin died instantly. However, when people turned to me and asked me why, I felt like I failed my family here.

I still have flashes of this night in my head that will probably be ingrained for a long time. One thing I have learned though is that we need prayer. We need a hedge of protection around this campus. I want to challenge you to pray for protection over this campus, the staff, and NVM on a daily basis.

When I spoke to Dr. Edmond and told her what happened I said, "we need our hospital built." Her answer back was, "no we all need more prayer." She said the amount of accidents NVM has been involved in over my last year here is not normal and we need more prayer.

18 APPENDIX 2

This past month, I also witnessed my first Voodoo "healing" ceremony. Although, I am not really sure what healing went on? A woman arrived on a motorcycle near the entrance of what some call the house of Satan. Four men met her outside and began spitting in her face. At first I was not sure what was going on. I thought they were going to beat her and I quickly thought, "what do I do, what do I do?" As I continued to watch they started pouring water all over her body and slapping her. Next, they took a torch and lit it on fire. They started circling her body with it, and touched both sides of her head and under her feet. It wasn't long after that they had her kneel down and I asked the people around me, "what are they doing to her?" They told me they were taking care of her, she is sick. I thought, well that sure seems funny.

As I continued to stare, I watched the head guy pull out a whip and start beating her. Confused and stunned I could not believe what was going on before my eyes. How could anyone think this is helping heal sickness? How could all the people standing around watching not think this was abnormal? After the whipping, they poured some more water or some type of liquid all over her again, showered her with dirt, and took her inside the temple. Everyone returned to what they were doing and it was as if nothing had ever happened. My mind kept spinning though; I wanted to know how anyone could think whipping someone would cure some ailment. However, I suppose if I heard the rationale behind what they were doing I would still disagree and think it's bogus.